Contemplating
the Holocaust

Contemplating
the Holocaust

Bernhard H. Rosenberg
Chaim Z. Rozwaski

JASON ARONSON INC.
Northvale, New Jersey
Jerusalem

This book was set in 11 pt. Galliard by Alabama Book Composition of Deatsville, AL and printed and bound by Book-mart Press, Inc. of North Bergen, NJ.

10 9 8 7 6 5 4 3 2

Library of Congress Cataloging-in-Publication Data

Rosenberg, Bernhard H.
Contemplating the holocaust / by Bernhard H. Rosenberg and
Chaim Z. Rozwaski.
        p.   cm.
ISBN 0–7657–6111–4
1. Holocaust, Jewish (1939–1945)   I. Rozwaski, Chaim Z.
II. Title.
D804.3.R69   1999
940.53′18—dc21   99–34348
                                                          CIP

Printed in the United States of America on acid-free paper. For information and catalog write to Jason Aronson Inc., 230 Livingston Street, Northvale, NJ 07647-1726, or visit our website: www.aronson.com

My wife, Charlene, joins me in dedicating this book to the memory of my beloved parents, Jacob and Rachel Rosenberg, of blessed memory, Holocaust survivors, and to our children, Yibadlu Ll'chaim Tovim V'arukhim, Ilana, Ayelet, Yaakov, and Ari.

—Bernard H. Rosenberg

My wife, Roberta, joins me in dedicating this book to my parents, David and Basia, and my infant brother, Yechiel Rozwaski, who perished in the Holocaust; and to our grandchildren, Yibadlu Ll'chaim Tovim V'arukhim, Eliezer Meir, Kayla Bracha, and Moshe Avraham Rozwaski, the children of my son and daughter-in-law Ahvner Aharon and Raizel Zlata Rozwaski; and to Menachem Mendel, Baruch Aryeh, and Tova Reichel Rephun, the children of my daughter and son-in-law, Batya Geela and Hesh Rephun.

—Chaim Z. Rozwaski

This book is dedicated to the memory of Rabbi Bernhard H. Rosenberg's parents, who survived the Holocaust, and to his children. It is co-authored by Rabbi Rosenberg. This book is dedicated to the memory of Rabbi Chaim Z. Rozwaski's parents and brother, who perished in the Holocaust, and to the grand-children of Rabbi Chaim Z. Rozwaski. It is co-authored by Rabbi Rozwaski, who is a Holocaust survivor himself.

We have before us three generations of post-Holocaust families. We can humbly say and pray that *Chut Hamshulash Lo Bim'hayra Yinatayk*—A threefold chain shall not easily be broken.

There is something of poetic justice in this event that can point only to the lesson that God's hand is directing the life of the Jewish people and guiding our destiny.

We take comfort in the fact that despite all odds against our being alive, let alone marrying and having children and grandchildren and writing books about our lives, we are privileged to bear witness to God's protection and blessings of the Jewish people. We praise Him to whom all praise is due for His mercy endures forever.

—BR, CR

Contents

Contents

Acknowledgments

We want to pay tribute to several of our friends and acknowledge the help they gave us in publishing this book. No creative work can be achieved without the encouragement and support of people around us. This is particularly true of a work that deals with painful memories and calls to mind our own responsibilities in keeping those painful memories alive. Any book on the *Shoah* is such a book. This book is particularly so because it expresses many views that are quite critical of the Jewish community and its handling of the *Shoah* today. It also makes many comments on the historical and theological perspectives of the *Shoah* from the Jewish point of view that are not politically correct today. We are therefore very grateful to our many friends for helping us with this publication and for the moral support they gave us in the process. We particularly want to acknowledge the help of Mr. and Mrs. Bernard (and Joan) Rubinstein, Maria Devinki, Sam Devinki, Frank S. Facchini, Jeffrey A. Fladell, David Halpern, Gary B. Rosen, Steven Edward Some, Adam Sprung, Paul D. Vartanian, Lillian Levitz Wertlieb, and Brandon Flynn, Sr. May God bless them with long life and *nachas* in their families. In helping us publish this book they have also helped to perpetuate the memory of those of our beloved people who have perished in the *Shoah, Hashem Yinkom et Damam Hashafuch.*

We also want to thank Arthur Kurzweil of Jason Aronson Inc. for his cooperation and interest in the publication of this book. The publication of this book took much time and effort involving discussion, consultation, and planning. We thank him for his efforts and guidance in publishing this book.

Finally, we thank our wives, Roberta Rozwaski and Charlene Rosenberg, and our children for their patience and support while we pursued this task and worked as rabbis of our respective pulpits. We also thank our congregants and friends of our congregations for giving us the opportunity to serve them and yet engage in this literary work. May God bless them and their dear ones.

God has been good to us. We are intractably intertwined with the *Shoah*. My parents, David and Basha Rozwaski, and infant baby brother, Yechiel, were murdered in the *Shoah* during the slaughter of the Jews of my birth town Zhettel, Poland. Jacob and Rachel Rosenberg, the parents of Rabbi Rosenberg, survived the *Shoah* with all the tragedy it entailed. We are fortunate to be alive, have families of our own, and be building a future while serving as leaders of our respective congregations and communities. For this we are eternally grateful to our God, the God of our fathers who was with us in the darkest days of our history and is with us now as we see the reemergence of a new Jewish life throughout the world. For all of this we humbly thank and praise our God, blessed be His Eternal name forever and ever.

Introduction

The essays in this book cover a wide variety of topics. They range from a survivor's very personal reflections and those of a son of survivors, to the nature of the press's response during the *Shoah* and the quest for the meaning of the tragedy of life. The essays deal with such questions as the lack of standard universal commemorative services by the Jewish communities, the continuing efforts by the Catholic Church to Christianize the *Shoah*, the commercialization of the *Shoah*, the attempt to de-emphasize the impact of the *Shoah* on the Jewish people, the historical way in which Jews commemorated their martyrs in the past, and the emergence of a Holocaust culture that serves as a surrogate for genuine Judaism. They deal with the silence of the world during the war years, the lessons from the *Shoah*, the way our dear ones died, the nature of Jewish resistance, and the Jews who survived but are lost to the Jewish people. The essays express a plea from the heart to all children to love their parents. The essays address the question of who speaks for the martyrs of the *Shoah*, how the martyrs went to their death, *Kristalnacht*, and many more subjects. Generally they are a reflection of the questions that trouble all those who are concerned with the ethical, political, and theological questions raised by the *Shoah*.

The *Shoah* will be with us for many years to come. However, as it recedes more and more into history it will be dealt with more and more in an impersonal, detached, and laboratory-like manner. The depersonalization of the Jew as a human being begun by the Nazi machine will be completed by the Holocaust historians who will, of course, work in the name of scientific objectivity. It is against this background that many of the essays have been written. They express a personal *crie de cour* of the writers at the lack of overall Jewish public concern about the *Shoah*, the direction the commemorative public observances are taking, the misrepresentation and politicization of the *Shoah* on the part of Jewish officialdom. The essays are an attempt to shed a more personal and historical light on the *Shoah*, the feelings it evokes, and the memories it brings to light.

These essays were not written lightly. They were written with pain and serious meditation. We wish that we would not have had to write about some of the topics and that some of the issues, such as the trends of the *Shoah* observances, the misinterpretation of the way out martyrs died, and so forth, would not have taken place. Unfortunately, these errors have become embedded in the social and historical fabric of the masses. The need to counteract this as well as present another view on these subjects—a view that is more in keeping with Judaism and the historical events as we know them—is what motivated us to write this book.

The essays in this book are not presented in any particular

order—they appear as they were written. That is not to say that the essays were not arranged in any particular form. Rather, they follow a free-ranging order. This serves to reflect the enormity of the different feelings and thoughts the *Shoah* brings out in so many people and indicates that the subject of the *Shoah* is so vast that it affects almost every aspect of our lives. The *Shoah* certainly has a tremendous impact on our emotions. Whether we are survivors, children of survivors, or Jews, and all Jews are survivors, we cannot be sanguine when it comes to the *Shoah*. No amount of trying to treat it as another event in history can avoid the trauma of the *Shoah*. Jews have become too involved and too much a part of Western life and history during the last century to be able to shrug off the *Shoah* as simply another episode of anti-semitism like that of the Middle Ages. And yet if it is not anti-semitism, then what is it? How can we explain its occurrence? How can we account for the miserable failure of Western civilization (of which we wanted and tried so hard and so much to become a part), to act in order to avert such an occurence? And, after the *Shoah*, can we still be a part of the civilization that tried to annihilate us, and if we can, should we? What can it offer us, ethically, morally, and culturally? Surely these must be the underlying questions gnawing away at every thinking person's conscience—Jew and non-Jew alike. Can any Jew who has any semblance of Jewish identity ever feel comfortable in the West? (We keep hearing that this is a new generation. But the same was said of the previous generation as well. Neither can it be said that the children of the previous generation were not different from their parents.) Can any Jew ever feel secure again? And are those who feel secure not misreading history and human nature and creating for themselves the illusion of security and acceptance?

The essays address some pertinent questions in history. They assert that the world did know and the press did not care, and people stood by and were essentially indifferent to the suffering, sorrow, death, and destruction of the Jews. Read the essays about the *New York Times* and the *London Times*, and *Mein Kampf* and others and you will learn how much the world knew and how little it cared.

The essays speak about what Jewish courage is all about. They tell us about the real heroism of the Jewish people, their dignity, and their faith in life and in death. Read and remember the essays, "Dignity and Resistance," "The Sanctification of God's Name," "The Threefold Nature of Jewish Resistance in the Days of the Shoah," and you will gain a new perspective of how Jews lived and died.

There is an array of additional topics that the essays touch upon but most of all they express a call for Jewish awareness of what the *Shoah* really was, of what it stands for in Jewish history, of what we ought to do to remember it, and finally we should always remember it with dignity and sorrow, with pride and *Yirath HaKavod*, (reverential respect) for our martyrs.

1

Remembering Whom?

There is an old dictum and hallowed custom that when speaking of the enemies of the Jewish people or of a wicked person, one says immediately after mentioning their names, *Yimach Shmo V'zichro*—may his name and memory be blotted out. There is no doubt that at no other time in our history has it been more urgent and necessary to adhere to this principle than in our time, and no one else deserved to be obliterated from our memory nor have his memory blotted out more than the German murderers and their collaborators who slaughtered six million Jewish people, from infants to old persons alike, as well as millions of other nationals throughout Europe. The need to preserve and pay homage to the memory of the Martyrs of the Holocaust raises a poignant question, "How do you commemorate the names of the Holocaust martyrs without also preserving the names and keeping alive the memory of their murderers?" Indeed, museums constructed to commemorate the Holocaust tend to equally memorialize the perpetrators of the heinous crimes of the Holocaust. One has only to walk into any Holocaust museum to see the pictures, memorabilia, and insignias of those perpetrators; and to see the vicious sadism on the faces of the butchers of the Jewish people, and the other human beings, on display side by side with their victims' pictures. Instead of obliterating their memory, the Holocaust museums inadvertently preserve it. And who knows and who can tell if some sick-minded individuals who walk into those museums are not moved, by some form of mental and emotional perversion, to imitate those wicked creatures of history, instead of holding them in contempt, despising their deeds and abhorring them? This is an ancient Jewish dilemma.

Ours is not the first generation of Jews that has had to wrestle with this question and to seek an answer to the painful problem of keeping the memory of our martyrs alive, and blotting out the names of our nemeses.

When God took the Jewish people out of Egyptian bondage, they thought that they were finally free and on their way to a new life. Instead, they were mercilessly attacked by the Amalekites who, Scripture tells us, particularly relished assaulting the weak and the struggling, those who fell behind and could not keep up with the march of the people. After centuries of bondage, the newly freed people were finally seeing the dawn of salvation and rays of sunshine entering their lives. When they saw their march toward freedom being cut short by the ferocious and unprovoked attack of the Amalekites, they were thrust once more onto the brink of disillusionment and despair. The onslaught of the Amalekite people upon our ancestors, coming from a nation that was itself under the yoke of Egyptian domination, and thus should have welcomed them with open arms instead of arrows and knives, must have been a severe blow, not only to the physical body, but also to the emotions and thinking of the newly emancipated Jewish people. Rabbinic tradition teaches us that the action of the Amalekites was seen not only as an attack against the Jews, but as a blow against God Himself and an act of defiance against God's design to save the Jews. Thus, the Amalekites not only attacked the Jews, but also attacked God. It is in this sense that the rabbis explain the unusually harsh Divine condemnation of the Amalekites by God and His pledge to ". . . utterly blot out the remembrance of Amalek from under heaven . . ." (Exodus 17:14). This commandment instructed the Jewish people to "Remember what Amalek did unto thee by the way as ye came forth out of Egypt; how he met thee by the way, and smote the hindmost of thee, all that were enfeebled in thy rear, when thou wast faint and weary; and he feared not God. Therefore it shall be, when the Lord thy God hath given thee rest from all thine enemies round about, in the land which the Lord thy God giveth thee for an inheritance, to possess it, that thou shalt blot out the remembrance of Amalek from under heaven; thou shalt not forget" (Deuteronomy 25:17–19) The Divine response to the dastardly behavior of Amalek was twofold; one, that God would remove the very memory of Amalek from the history of mankind, and two, that the Jews should do the same, by His command.

The question arises, "How do you blot out a name when you are constantly reminded to do so? Don't you in the very act of blotting that name out also recall it, and thus, in trying to erase it, actually perpetuate its memory?" Put in other words, how is it possible to talk about the victim without mentioning the victimizer at the same time? Our ancestors then had the same problem that we have now.

Many years after the Egyptian Exodus, when the Jews were

once more threatened with extermination, in this case by Haman, (who, according to tradition was a descendent of Amalek), and came out victoriously from that confrontation, they were instructed by their leaders, Mordechai and Esther, to commemorate that event also. (Esther 9:20–28). To this day, Jews everywhere celebrate the Festival of Purim in commemoration of the defeat of Haman and his cohorts, and in fulfillment of Mordechai's and Esther's instructions. The main feature of the observance of the Festival of Purim is to read the Scroll of Esther on the eve and the morning of the day of Purim. One of the episodes of the saga of Purim mentioned in the Scroll of Esther is the story of the hanging of Haman's ten sons. When their names are mentioned, we are instructed by the rabbinic rules governing the laws of reading the Scroll of Esther to quickly run through all the ten names in *one breath*. In actuality their names should not be mentioned at all. To do that is impossible since it would entail the elimination of a passage from Scripture. Therefore, the next best thing to omitting their names is to utter them as quickly as one possibly can in one breath, which is as good as not mentioning them at all. Thus their memory is blotted out while Scripture is kept inviolate.

We may reasonably conclude that our ancestors in the days of Mordechai and Esther were confronted with a similar predicament of trying to perpetuate the memory of the events that befell them on the one hand, and to blot out the memory of the wicked people on the other. They solved the problem by subduing any reference to the perpetrators of evil, and where possible, omitting any reference to them all together. And whenever any mention of them was unavoidable, they made sure that their names were mentioned with derision and scorn and were held up as an example of wickedness that is forever to be condemned and rejected by God fearing people. Thus when the Scroll of Esther is being read, not only are the names of Haman's sons disposed of as quickly as possible but each time Haman's name is mentioned, it is followed by shouts of booing and noisemaking, which make it almost impossible for the name to be heard, as a sign of disapproval and a means of obliterating it entirely.

There may be a telling lesson in this practice for us in our quest for a way out of the dilemma of trying to commemorate the Holocaust martyrs, while at the same time omitting any reference to those evil creatures who created the Holocaust.

Holocaust museums must not stop at the display of the outrageous atrocities that were committed by the Germans and their collaborators (as we should not stop at the recitation of the proverbial platitude "never again," nor be content with proclamations that we must not idly stand by and watch atrocities being committed even now throughout the world). Instead, the museums must ensure that displays of Nazi and German war symbols, insignia, pictures of German soldiers and war paraphernalia and all contact with the German war machine, especially such items as may show them in a heroic fashion, should be avoided at all cost. Whenever such displays are unavoidable, they should be accompanied by explanations and condemnations of the evil that they represent. Next to each display of pictures or insignias there should be a call to all humankind to abhor and reject the evil that these symbols represent.

We can solve the problem of the painful paradox that confronts us every time we try to remember our martyrs of the *Shoah*. The paradox is that we want to remember them and forget they are murderers; yet every time we think of them, we have to mention they are murderers also. The lesson of Purim has shown us a way out. Even though it is almost humanly impossible to separate the two from each other, it is possible to put a great distance between them by denouncing the evil deeds of the Germans and their collaborators, by referring to them by word or picture as little as possible, and by constantly denouncing and condemning them and their actions. It is also important to emphasize the triumph of good over evil, and of right over might, and to teach at all times that those who take up evil as their cause in life take death into their hands and seal their own fate of obliteration from the book of human history. At every sign of, and reference to, those who created the *Shoah* there must also be a proclamation that those who choose evil as their way of life, choose to confront God, and that those who attack their fellow human beings, attack God. God created humankind to live, and those who would deny them life deny God's plan. As the remembrance of Amalek, who attacked God by attacking the Jewish people, is to be blotted out from under the heavens, so are they to be blotted out from the memory of humankind.

—*CR*

2

The Christianization of the Holocaust

The surge on the part of so many people of different nationalities to claim the status of Holocaust victims of German bestiality during World War II, and at the very same time, to deny the fact that the Jews are the only ones who have a right to claim the so-called distinction of having been the sole victims of the Holocaust, must be one of the most startling events of the post World War II era and indeed in the annals of human history. It is hard to find another case where those who participated in perpetrating the crime of civilization on another people unashamedly claim to be its own victims. It is truly amazing! It is as though after the Jews have been destroyed physically, an attempt is now made to destroy them spiritually. After annihilating their bodies, they now want to destroy their memories too! When the Jews were killed, they stood all alone. Now when they are dead, everyone wants to be part of them! What is the reason for this rush to identify with the Jewish victims? What does that mean for the Jews and what does it tell us about the people of these nationalities?

To answer these questions, we must first understand what the whole issue of the Holocaust means to these nations, the Christian world, and particularly the Vatican. Above all else, the Holocaust serves as a mirror image of western man and particularly those who were involved in the European war theater during World War II. It is the revelation, on the morning after awakening from the horrifying nightmare that mankind experienced during the horrible night of World War II, that it was not a dream at all, but the naked truth. The truth is hard to face.

What is the truth?

The truth is that the Holocaust was an attempt to annihilate all the Jews from the face of the earth. Wherever the German hand of conquest reached, there the Jews were exterminated. The policy of making the world *Judenrein* applied to all the world. It was not limited to Europe alone. It was only delayed and not implemented in practice due to, one, the slowness of the pace of conquest, two, the obvious resistance to the Germans on the part of the nations about to be conquered, and finally, the Allied victory. The truth is that all the occupied nations (with the exception of tiny Denmark) collaborated with the Germans in their attempt to annihilate the Jews. Toward the end of the war that also included Japan, though with some resistance, the main organizations and groups involved in the organized life of the occupied countries went along with the German policy and program of exterminating the Jews. Indeed they participated in this gruesome and cruel effort. Without their support and cooperation the Germans would not have succeeded the way, and as much as, they did. That is not to deny but, per contra, to emphasize the fact that in each occupied country there were heroic men and women who risked their lives and in some cases, paid with their lives, to save and help Jews. Indeed, were it not for these men and women, the few Jews who did survive might never have lived through the war. The heroism and sheer selfless humanitarianism of these kind and noble people were made that much greater and heroic in the face of the constant threats of being informed on, arrested by or turned over to the police by their own neighbors, relatives, friends and members of the community. The torturous fear of one's own countrymen was greater than the fear of the Germans. If the general population would only have remained passive and not cooperated with the Germans in their policy to kill the Jews, the righteous Gentiles would have saved that many more Jews; fewer righteous Gentiles would have been killed trying to save Jews, and at the end more Jews would have been alive today. But this did not happen because the governments and the populations of the occupied countries cooperated fully with the Germans in the extermination of the Jews.

The truth is that most of the existing religious, social, cultural, and professional organizations and guilds, indeed all the groups that continued to function under German occupation, did not resist the German destruction of their fellow Jews. On the contrary, they cooperated with the Germans in the destruction of the Jewish people. This is the case of the average organization. In addition to this, add the fact of the well-known fascist-collaborating political parties, youth groups and anti-Semitic clubs and organizations that existed in each of the countries even before they were occupied by Germany. Under German occupation, these groups let loose with their previously controlled hatred and their vicious handiwork of the devil against the Jews and anyone that would help them. Now you might have a picture of the truth of the environment in and circumstances under which the Jews struggled to survive.

The truth is that the religious groups, that is, the churches of all denominations, who had the greatest moral influence on the people of Eastern Europe, as a whole also collaborated with the Germans in destroying the Jews.

The only ones who helped the Jews were kindhearted individuals of all backgrounds, personal friends, relatives by marriage, individual priests from all denominations, some nationalistic resistance movements and their members, and the communists. Some of these people did it on humanistic grounds, others for money, some for ideological motives, others for personal reasons, such as love, and some as a means of fighting the Germans. Helping the Jews was not a priority on the list of any one of these organizations. No one organization can say that it made helping the Jews a priority of its mission and reason for existing.

The truth is that when Jews managed, by the grace of God, to escape the Germans, they were killed by their neighbors and/or their fellow citizens.

The truth is that all the nations of Europe collaborated and worked with the Germans in killing the Jews. In some ways they even surpassed the Germans in brutality and cruelty.

The truth is that millions of people from the occupied countries volunteered to serve in the German armies and fought on all fronts, be it the Russian, the western, or in Normandy against the landing forces of the allied armies on D-Day. The truth is that the bulk, perhaps as many as eighty to ninety percent, of the people from Russia, Poland, Ukraine, Estonia, Latvia, Lithuania, Romania, Hungary, Czechoslovakia and others who ended up in the Displaced Persons camps of Germany and other places in Western Europe following the war in 1945, were German collaborators. They ran from their native countries for fear of retribution by their own fellow countrymen who knew their true nature and what they did together with the Germans. Having escaped the wrath of their countrymen and with the start of the Cold War, they found it convenient to hide under the umbrella of running from communism.

The truth is these people never atoned for their evil deeds. They never recanted. They were never punished for their wickedness. Instead they came to the Displaced Persons camps and claimed the pity and compassion that was due the victims. They turned the facts of history upside down. They became the victims.

Thanks to the Cold War, it worked. It worked so well that they were able to migrate to all the free countries and join in the pursuit of the good life without any encumbrances, except for those inherent in their native ability and talent.

The truth is that these people would not have been able to perpetrate this hoax and fraud that turned history on its head if it were not for the cooperation of many, many organizations, the Allied governments, and above all, the Roman Catholic Church, which far and beyond all other organizations should have called out for truth. Forget justice! Forget just and deserved punishment! Forget vengeance! Welcome mercy! Proclaim forgiveness! But never, never cover up the truth! We must ask, "Shall the church who prides itself in having the truth, and proclaims from the rooftops, "Veritas!" and shouts to the whole world, "The truth shall set you free," hide the truth?

The truth is that for the western world as a whole and the church in particular, the truth of the Holocaust is too heavy a burden to carry. It is its cross that it shall never be able to unburden and free itself of.

At the conclusion of World War II the whole world was in a state of moral shock. It was in a state of numbing stupor. The world was aghast to see the devastation of the war, the horrors of the concentration camps and the extermination of millions of Jews, which took place in the presence and in the midst of the silence of an entire Western world, and was perpetrated by and under the leadership of Germany, the most scientifically, technologically and culturally advanced state in the history of European civilization. The Allied world was further dismayed to learn that the Vatican, which prides itself on being the moral conscience of the world and the most significant spokesman of the Christian world at that, was thunderously silent, at best, and, at worst, a tacit collaborator of the German occupation forces. Thus it gave silent approval to the horrendous German crimes against God and man. This led immediately after World War II not only to a period of disillusionment with religion as such, but also to a serious questioning of the role of the Vatican in World War II, its relationship with Germany, and particularly its moral and political position on the attempted extermination of the Jews.

World War II left the Christian world in a state of moral impotence and theological confusion. But the biggest question mark was raised over the Vatican, "Where were you during World War II?" To this question there was no answer. This indeed presented the religious community with the greatest challenge to its moral and theological authority in the last two thousand years, or since the rise of Christianity as a world religion. As long as this question went unanswered, the moral authority of the church was threatened with continually remaining under a big question mark. The Vatican in particular was to remain forever under a dark cloud of doubt about its integrity as a religious authority in the world, and without its moral integrity, it could not long survive as the symbol of a world religion of the highest magnitude, which it claimed to be. The best defense of its moral turpitude during World War II was to claim that it too was a victim and therefore in no position to do anything. In an age when the whole world was up in flames, it was not difficult to point to many burning houses. Indeed, there were some clergy of all denominations who helped the victims, Jewish and non-Jewish alike; who resisted German atrocities and murder and stood up for liberty and human kindness. These people who acted as individuals, often even in fear of and against the orders of their own superiors, now became the heroes of the church. Their sacrifice now served as the flag under which the church proclaimed that it was a fighter for freedom and champion of anti-German resistance.

This trend on the part of the church to identify itself with the victims of World War II continued slowly for many years until gradually, the church began to claim that it too was part of the Holocaust. Finally, this process of first identifying with and then replacing the victim reached its apex with the construction of the monastery on the grounds of the Auschwitz Extermination Camp.

Constructing a monastery and turning it into a residence of the Carmelite nuns on the very soil that is soaked with the blood of the Jewish victims of the Holocaust was nothing short of an attempt to turn the history of the Holocaust on its head. In one move the church turned from victimizer to victim. With one bold stroke, the Catholic Church created a fact that, were it not reversed by the outcry of the Jewish activists and those who dealt in quiet diplomacy with the Vatican, would have elevated the church from being a tacit partner to the perpetration of the Holocaust, to that of being its innocent victim. In this way, it strove to retain its role in history as the bearer of the divine message of moral authority, religious integrity and social justice in the world.

The Holocaust is and forever will remain the cross that the church will have to bear. For the Holocaust is the mirror of the world. It reflects the true nature and soul of man. For all eternity, all thinking men will be able look at this mirror and see who, in the long history of mankind, is the real harbinger of peace, and who of violence; who is the genuine suffering servant of God, and who is his adversary; who speaks with the authentic voice of the moral authority that comes from Sinai and who does not.

The church will respond now to the questions, "Where were you during the war?" in the way it responded to the victims during the dark days of the Holocaust—with silence! It will have nothing to say. Its dark record will speak for itself. Thus the moral failure of the church during the Holocaust carries within itself the potential undoing of the church in general and the Vatican in particular. The only way the Vatican can redeem itself from this moral failure is to acknowledge this failure totally, and to try to correct itself by changing its entire system of education, theological instruction, and relationship with other religions. (Some argue that this is what it is trying to do.) But as a whole, it seems to have chosen another path. The church denies its role during the Holocaust. It is attempting to stall and also in the meantime, change the facts of history by becoming a victim, claiming also to be a casualty of the Holocaust. It seeks to identify with Holocaust projects and become a part of an emerging Holocaust theology of redemption. That is, by using the theme of the Holocaust as a way to address current crimes against humanity that are being perpetrated around the world, the church appeals to the conscience of humankind in the name of the Holocaust and thereby further dilutes the innate Jewishness of the Holocaust. Following this road of denial, identification with, and replacement of the real victims of the Holocaust—the Jews—the Vatican hopes to regain and retain its moral and religious leadership in the world.

We can now turn to the original question, "Why are so many people of different nationalities claiming to be the victims of the Holocaust? The answer is now clear. They do this to further deny Jews the claim to heroism that they nobly displayed during the dark night of the Holocaust. These people do this to cover up their own guilt during the war. The people who claim to be the newly discovered victims of the Holocaust are the Poles, the Ukrainians, the Latvians, the Estonians, and the Lithuanians. These are the people with the most blood on their hands. They were the greatest collaborators with the Germans. They have the most to answer for.

Their conscience is troubled the most. They have to answer the question all mankind asks. They have to answer the question their children and their children's children will keep on asking to the end of days. As long as they keep professing to be good God fearing Christians, they will be haunted by the question, "Where were you during World War II?" To avoid the terrible trauma of conscience brought on by this question, they point an accusing finger to a bewildered world. They follow the example of the church and are shading their own past and taking on the new identity of the old Jew who was killed by them. They now claim to be the Jew. By replacing the Jew as a victim and taking his place, they not only deny their own culpability as participants in the perpetration of the Holocaust, but also deny that the Jew was the victim. They remove his presence as a factor in the story of the Holocaust. Thus they erase the memory of the victimized Jew and pave the way for a new history of World War II and the saga of the Holocaust.

The attempt to join the ranks of the Jews as victims of the Holocaust and to deny the Jews the status of being the sole and only victims of World War II who have the right to claim that they, and only they, are the sole victims of the Holocaust, is to pave the way for the whitewashing of the nefarious role of the Vatican, the church as a whole, and the peoples of the occupied countries in the German plan to exterminate the Jews from the face of the earth. It sets the stage for a future rewriting of history, a history in which the church is going to claim the main role of having been the great spiritual and heroic antagonist of Germany during the time of the Holocaust. The basis for this rewriting of history and preempting for the Vatican the role of the great champion of human rights, social justice and the towering moral and religious human leader in the struggle against the German attempt to annihilate Western civilization (imbedded in what has become known as the Judeo-Christian tradition) was laid in the building of the monastery in Auschwitz. This is the most perfidious and cunning attempt to rewrite history in order to serve the interest of the Vatican and destroy the moral status and righteous message inherent in the Holocaust of the Jews.

—CR

3

They Went Like Sheep
to the Slaughter
and Other Myths

To march silently into the gas chambers, to line up against a wall waiting for the bullet that would end life, or to stand naked at the edge of a ravine filled with bloodied, lifeless bodies, awaiting one's turn to die, is beyond comprehension. It defies what we know of man' s overwhelming desire to survive against all odds.

Indelibly printed in the minds of not only the survivors and their children, but in the minds of people everywhere, are the questions, "Why didn't they fight?" and "Why did they go like sheep to the slaughter?"

Not true! A gross falsehood! It is our enemies' conclusion

that the Jews, who are indeed different to start with, were neither brave nor courageous, and that they were accepting just punishment for crimes they had committed The Warsaw ghetto uprising was not an imaginary episode dreamed up by cowards. It was stark reality sparked and executed by courageous heroes and martyrs.

One had but to search their faces to see that these were people with no hope. Betrayed and abandoned by the world and by mankind as well, they were left to grope in darkness and terror. Make no mistake. The responsibility for their extermination lies not in their lack of courage, but solely with the Nazis and their collaborators.

There are no pat answers to some obvious questions that arise concerning the Holocaust. One needs time to read, research, discuss and reflect upon all the available diversified material relating to this infamous period in the history of man. One certainly needs time to speak to the "returnees from Hitler's hell," the survivors. Because many of us do not have such time at our disposal, I would like to clarify one painful, shame-filled issue by attempting to analyze "sheep to the slaughter."

We must try to walk in the victim's shoes, crawl into his skin, and take on his identity. Jews of the Holocaust began to know terror as part of daily living, with the Nuremberg Laws, anti-semitic newspaper articles, broadcasts, rallies, beatings and economic boycotts, all part of the process to dehumanize him.

How much can he withstand? Jumbled thoughts meander in his head. Should he take his wife and his children and flee Europe? How could he leave his aging parents and beloved family behind? Will he be able to get out? Where should he run? Where could he go when the International Conference at Evian, France, has demonstrated that he is unwanted, that no country will accept Jews. The doors to freedom and, therefore, to life are closed to the victim. There are no keys. Like a pariah, a leper, shunned and unwanted elsewhere, trapped, his passport is now stamped with the letter "J" for "Jude." *Kristalnacht* finds Nazis wantonly destroying homes, businesses and shuls in his town, inhuman deeds orchestrated by hate for the purpose of eradicating all signs of Jewish life.

Now it begins in earnest. His friends are arrested, interrogated, beaten and sent to concentration camps. His precious children are expelled from school. He is unable to explain why they are living a nightmare and cannot allay their fears. He is forced to wear the yellow badge of death and his home is confiscated. He must now live in a ghetto.

Seven in one small room, insufficient food to sustain life, little or no medication available to cope with illness, he watches helpless, as Jews of all ages die in the streets. One of his children becomes ill and succumbs. He wails in anguish but the world is deaf and uncaring.

Then the day arrives when he is told to report to the railroad station with his family; and he must obey. During the unspeakable five day trip in boxcars, his father expires gasping for air. The dead are not permitted the luxury of falling but are held upright, pressed against the living like sardines.

Faint with hunger, barely conscious, they arrive at a concentration camp and are processed immediately. The victim is parted from his family by a small beast wearing a Nazi uniform. In his hand is a whip with which he points to the left or to the right, prolonging or ending life. The Jew soon learns that many of his loved ones have perished in the "ovens" yet *he* tenaciously clings to life.

He is witness to death, torture and unbelievable acts of degradation at the hands of the Nazi monsters. Like a haunted animal, he begins to think only of his survival. He exists from hour to hour trying to be invisible in order to avoid more suffering. He dreams of escape. Escape how? Escape to where? In this hell where the labor is unbearable, the hunger forever gnawing at his insides, he becomes plagued by nightmares in which he sees his wife and children gasping for air in the gas chambers, sees his mother's outstretched arms begging for rachmonis and his neighbor, Moishe, beaten to death. He can't quiet his children's voices, the reality of which awakens him night after night. He tries in vain to eradicate the thoughts concerning the horrors being performed, in the name of science, on the Jewish women; and with all this, he does not cry. He has no tears left.

Yet there are moments of sanity and he dares to hope that this will end so that he will be free of pain and hunger and shame. He even dreams sometimes that he will arise from the slime, a whole man, a man who will build a new life. How dare the world ask "Why didn't they fight back?", "Why didn't they kill the guards?", "Why did they go like sheep to the slaughter?" Fight back with what? How? Broken in body, weary to death in spirit, how could our victim fight?

The world must learn that bravery and courage take many forms and that the Holocaust victims lacked for neither. The will to survive, to rejoin the human race that had abandoned them, to build a new life and a better world for others, that takes special courage. By virtue of surviving and crawling back from the filth, morass and horror of Hitler's hell, they fought back. They are unsung heroes who lived to alert mankind to the unspeakable evils that live in man, evils nourished by hatred and prejudice.

The flickering wick of Jewish life could not be extinguished by the Nazi monsters. The story of the Holocaust must be told again and again so that our children, our children's children and their children will know that the Jews have been tyrannized, murdered, beaten, threatened, maligned, abased and degraded by enemies, for centuries. They did not, they cannot and will not destroy us!

The Holocaust happened! Six million Jews, our brothers, were exterminated! The world stood by and let it happen! We must instill our youth with pride in their Jewish heritage. They must be told the truth, that Jews have fought against tyranny for themselves as well as for others—always.

—BR

4

Did They Fight Back?

As a child of survivors of the Nazi death camps who has published extensive articles and editorials regarding the Holocaust, I am deeply disturbed and sense the deep pangs of anguish of those who still cannot either comprehend or appreciate the true acts of heroism that prevailed. As a practicing rabbi who refuses to allow the memories of the past to be distorted, I appeal to our fellow Jews. "Never forget the acts of heroism which made it possible for us to exist."

The recurring questions that haunt survivors and their children echo through the halls of time: "Why didn't they fight back? Why did they enter the chambers of death like sheep to the slaughter?" By our standards, such actions as placidly lining up against a wall to be shot, or walking silently into the gas chamber, or standing nude and obedient at the edge of a ravine filled with blood-covered bodies awaiting one's own turn to die, defy all understanding. Indeed, anti-Semites would suggest that Jews were different, somehow not quite as brave, not quite as courageous as the average person. Our enemies will even conclude that the Jews were guilty of the crimes they were accused of, and hence with heavy conscience and accepting the punishment for their "crimes," the Jews quietly submitted to their deserved punishment. Nothing could be a greater falsification of the truth. The hopelessness seen in their faces was not a reflection of guilt; rather it was a realization that they had been completely deserted and completely betrayed by humanity. The light of morality, conscience and brotherhood had been completely extinguished and for them life became a terror-filled abyss. Responsibility for their death lies clearly with the Nazis and their collaborators.

Individuals confronted by the Holocaust often ask obvious questions to which there are no simplistic answers. One needs to read, to study, to discuss, to reflect, and to interview individuals who have lived through the tortures of hell on earth. Since it is evident that many will not read the volumes necessary for research, allow us to attempt to analyze the crucial and sensitive issue of "sheep to the slaughter."

In order to understand the Jew of the Holocaust, we must attempt to put ourselves in his place. He knew of centuries of persecution carried out by the drunk and the sober, by the church and by government dictum. He had suffered many instances of prejudice, degradation, and depersonalization prior to the Holocaust. The Holocaust begins with the Nuremberg Laws, anti-semitic newspaper articles, cartoons, radio broadcasts, rallies, humiliations, beatings, intimidations and economic boycott. The Holocaust victim begins to feel as if he were choking; fear begins to be a part of daily life.

Maybe he should leave Europe, he thinks, but to where, and should he not stay together with his family? The International Conference at Evian, France, demonstrates that the world does not want the Jew. Not one country is willing to open the doors of freedom. The victim is trapped, like a child in a cage with a ravenous lion. The victim's passport is marked with the letter "J" for "Jude," and *Kristalnacht* results in vast destruction; his home, his shop and even his place of worship cannot escape the wrath of maniacs bent upon the complete annihilation of the Jewish faith.

Some Jews are arrested and sent to concentration camps and the victim is informed that his children are expelled from school. The children do not understand, the victim is powerless to explain these atrocities to them. A yellow badge is to be worn; to be found without it means death.

The innocent victim and his family are uprooted and resettled in a ghetto; seven people in a room, little food, almost no medicine. The old and the young perish in the street. The victim's child falls ill and dies. He cries and screams in anguish. He is helpless to save her. A four-month-old baby perishes and the world remains silent.

His family is ordered to report to the train station. On the journey there are no sanitary facilities; pressed together like sardines, the corpses have no room to fall. They stand like the rest for nine days. The victim's grandfather dies begging for air.

Finally, the concentration camp. They arrive ravenous with hunger, nearly unconscious. Here a short man motions with his finger to the left or to the right. The victim goes to the right; his family to the left. He soon discovers that the only means of escape is through the chimney.

His family, his wife, and his two children are already in the next world. The chimney continues operating at full capacity. The heart and the soul of the world remains uncompassionate.

An inmate attempts to overcome a guard. He is tortured brutally and hung in front of the inmates. Each victim begins thinking to himself that he wants to avoid that suffering. Revolt is meaningless, and even if he escaped, where would he go? No one wants him.

Each day brings unbearable hard work, maddening hunger, insults, beatings and degradation. Sickness is rewarded with poisonous injections and friends and family disappear in the early selection. Living has become hell on earth; he is tattooed like a branded calf, freezing in winter and boiling in summer. The pain is constant and there appears no relief in sight.

The victim dreams and longs for a better world. He yearns for the time to come when he will no longer suffer and will begin to rebuild anew. The world remains silent to his pleas. His dreams remain unfulfilled. His heroic vision of hope for the future is clouded by the reality of the inferno surrounding him. He is tormented by re-occurring nightmares. He hears the voices of his children, his wife, his parents and loved ones. He remembers the sight of Joseph, his friend and neighbor, who was buried alive. In front of his eyes stand Yaakov, his uncle, who was disemboweled, Chaim, who was hanged, and Chana, who was subjected to medical experiments and then tortured to death. Tears flow as he envisions Pinchas, who was drowned, and his brother, who was trampled to death. He awakens scarred by the memory of Shmuel, who was burnt with cigarettes, and then thrown into the burning crematorium while still alive.

Today the world has the audacity to exclaim "Why didn't they fight back?" "Why didn't they rush the armed guards?" "Why didn't they attempt mass suicide?" The world refuses to realize that courage and heroism are often expressed in an individual's will to live, to seek to survive and build a better life, a better world for himself and his future family. The world dares to forget that numerous heroic uprisings did occur. In reality, displays of courage and self-sacrifice were evident in individual acts of heroism. This the world refuses to remember.

The remnants of Hitler's inferno came back from the grave to build a new nation, a nation conceived in blood and tears, a nation that loudly proclaims, "I will not be silent. Jews return to your own home. Our gates are eagerly awaiting you." These survivors dedicated themselves and their children to a new purpose; the atrocities of the past, the inhumanity of mankind, could not extinguish the Jewish spirit.

Our young must be told that we have always fought tyranny. We did not die like sheep for the slaughter. The Jewish nation has experienced the inferno of humanity. Jews have been criticized, labeled, stereotyped and maligned, we have experienced anguish and peril. Many have tried to murder us; others to missionize our young and yet, through it all, we, unlike any other people, have survived.

Sophisticated twentieth century mechanistic society not only wishes to forget the atrocities of the Holocaust, but tragically wishes to deny that it ever existed. Professor Arthur Butz and his followers would have us believe that the Nazi extermination of six million Jews was a myth created by the Jewish stablishment. The tears and frequent nightmares of terror experienced by survivors, are these exaggerations exploited by Zionists? Are the numbers branded on the arms of survivors beauty marks, reminders of the good old days when orchestras played such melodic tunes as "Arbeit Macht Frei?"

The gas chambers of yesteryear have been replaced with sophisticated mind-controlling devices. Organized cults are directing their deceptive ploys against Jewish children. These evangelists robe themselves with creative labels such as Hare Krishna, Jews for Jesus and Moonies. These antagonists are deceptive, their prime target is our youth.

The propaganda machine rings aloud with the deceptions

of Hitler's *Mein Kampf.* Twentieth century anti-Semites declare that Jews control industry; that Jews operate the banks, direct Wall Street and manipulate the economy. These anti-Semites suggest that we control the mass media and that newspapers echo Jewish propaganda.

We Jews have been gassed in the bathhouses of humanity, burned in crematoria constructed by the world's intellectuals, our children bayonetted, their blood spilt on the walls of the most civilized nations in the world. We have returned from the grave. We did not perish in the inferno. Our nation will never march like sheep to the slaughter. The people of Israel shall live.

—BR

5

Kristalnacht Must Never Be Forgotten

Imagine one morning that you and your family are awakened by shouts and screams. Suddenly, the police break into your house. They start breaking the china, destroying the furniture, and shattering windows while showing great satisfaction in their destruction. Then you and your family are told to get dressed and are taken to the police station for no apparent reason. On the way, you see your synagogue in flames, and your neighbors throwing rocks at it.

This happened early in the morning, on November 9, 1938, to Miriam Cohn, a Jewish social worker who lived in Essen, Germany. In addition to Ms. Cohn, other, similar incidents occurred to other Jews who lived in Germany and Austria during the night of November 9, 1938, and the following day. During that night in 1938, mobs burned synagogues, destroyed Jewish homes and businesses, vandalized Jewish hospitals, orphanages and cemeteries, and dragged thousands of Jewish men, women and children into the streets, where they were beaten and humiliated. The Germans later called this night *Kristalnacht*—The Night of Broken Glass—because of the tons of shattered glass that scattered throughout German cities after it had taken place. The Jews began to call that date the beginning of the Holocaust because of the tremendous violence that started on that night and that grew even more dreadful as time had passed.

On November 7, 1938, the third secretary of the German Embassy in Paris, Ernst Vom Rath, was murdered by Herschel Grynzpan, a seventeen-year-old German-Jewish refugee. Herschel wanted to avenge his parents' expulsion, together with 15,000 other Polish Jews, from Germany to Zbonszym. The Nazis used the murder as an excuse to start the mobs and riots that began the "final solution," the extermination of the Jews.

The German government attempted to disguise the violence of those two days as a spontaneous protest on the part of the Aryan population. But in reality, *Kristalnacht* was organized by the Nazi chiefs and their thugs with technical skill and precision. The Nazi chiefs commanded the Gestapo and the storm troopers to incite mob riots throughout Germany and Austria.

Kristalnacht marked the beginning of the plan, to rob the Jews of their possessions for the benefit of the Reich, and then to sweep them forever from the German scene. Furthermore, thereafter, Jews had no place in the German economy, and no independent Jewish life was possible, with the dismissal of cultural and communal bodies, and the banning of the Jewish press.

During the week after *Kristalnacht*, the Jewish Telegraphic

Agency's Berlin reporter called the night "the worst outbreak of anti-Jewish violence in modern German history."

During *Kristalnacht*, over 1,100 synagogues were destroyed, as well as 7,500 Jewish businesses and countless Jewish homes. Several hundred Jews were killed and 30,000 were arrested and sent to the concentration camps at Sachsenhausen, Buchenwald and Dachau, where thousands more died.

Ronald Lauder, a former United States Ambassador to Austria and head of a foundation that has spearheaded *Kristalnacht* commemorations around the country said, "There is no date in the whole Holocaust like November 9, 1938. It showed for the first time the horror of what the Nazis were planning."

Today, many historians can trace a pattern of events, occurring before that night, that would suggest that such an atrocity would happen. In 1933, when the Nazis took power, German anti-semitism adopted quasi-legal forms. One of the new anti-Jewish forms of action, which had began with the Nuremberg Laws of 1935, included the separation of the Jews from the daily structure of German life. The Jews, systematically, were deprived of their civil rights; they were isolated from the general populace through humiliating identification measures. The Nazis boycotted the Jewish shops and took away their jobs. Then they made the Jews declare the value of their possessions. The civil service and the police often arrested the Jews and forced them to sell their property for a pittance.

One may ask how the entire world could stand by and allow such a disaster to occur. The fascist or authoritative regimes in Italy, Rumania, Hungary and Poland were governments that approved of this pogrom, and wanted to use the pogrom as a case to make their own anti-semitic policies stronger in their individual countries. The three Great Western powers—Great Britain, France and the United States—said the appropriate things but did nothing to save the Jews. Hitler, in the late 1930's, told the world to take the Jews, but no one was willing to take them.

Even in our own country, President Roosevelt and his administration kept expressing shock over the terrible events that were occurring in Germany and Austria, but when it came time to act and help save the refugees by bringing them to the United States, the United States government refused and replied that they had no intention of allowing more immigrants to enter the United States.

Looking back at Jewish history, we draw the lesson that every Jew should tread with caution and be alert to any hints of anti-semitism that might creep up in the public statements by any of our public and non-public officials now. In a powerful speech before members of the New York Jewish Civil Service organization, Former Ambassador Ronald S. Lauder warned that the ignorance and fear that bred anti-semitism in Hitler's Third Reich is being encouraged once again. "Today in America, we hear . . . those same charges," he commented. "There are those who tell us that Jews control the banks and the press. There are those who would tell us that Jews control Congress and the government. *Kristalnacht* teaches us many things, among them that we must remain vigilant and not permit even the smallest seed of anti-semitism to take root. We cannot afford to be complacent in the face of anti-semitic distortions. Quiet little lies grow to be big loud lies," the Ambassador remarked.

Some examples of the seeds of anti-semitism that Ambassador Lauder referred to are the Ku Klux Klan movement and the skinheads. As George Santayana wrote in *The Life of Reason*, "Those who cannot remember the past are condemned to repeat it."

—BR

6

Where Was the World's Conscience?

As the winds of Europe carried the stench of burning flesh, where was the world's conscience? The ovens of Auschwitz no longer burn, yet several burning questions about the Holocaust or World War II still remain. Who was responsible for the death of six million Jews during the Holocaust? The obvious answer is the one you and I have learned from our social studies teachers and from our history books. We say, "It was Hitler and his Nazi regime." Our history books and our teachers were not totally incorrect when they explained this to us, but perhaps they were not totally correct in their explanation either. We were told that, for the greater part of the war, the United States and the

Allied powers remained "neutral." Our teachers used words like "isolationist policy" and talked with us about the importance of keeping the United States out of the war. I want you to think about a more difficult question. Are not the bystanders as guilty as the perpetrators of this mass murder? Questions like this one and six million unanswered cries reveal the shocking realities of Allied neutrality, but more importantly, they reveal how the governments of the United States and the Allied powers must share the blame for the largest genocide in human history.

I am going to give you the rest of the story—the part your history books and social studies teachers left out—the part about how the United States and the Allied governments were accomplices to Hitler in the crimes committed against the Jewish people during World War II.

Let us first look at the United States immigration policy. During the Holocaust the United States had the most stringent immigration laws in the world. In fact, the laws were so strict, the United States did not even fill its own quotas. In the ten years between 1933 and 1943, the United States could have admitted more than a million and a half refugees, but chose to admit only a small percentage of that quota. One New York congressman remarked, "Not since 1862 have there been fewer aliens entering the United States. . . . It takes months to grant a visa, and then it usually applies to a corpse."

The United States denied entrance even to those refugees who held United States immigration numbers. In May of 1939, a ship called the St. Louis sailed from Nazi Germany to Cuba. After Cuba changed its mind and decided not to take in the refugees, whom they had previously promised to accept, the 734 refugees who held United States immigration numbers thought that the United States might take them in ahead of their projected time. The United States sent the ship and all the refugees back to Nazi Germany.

Do you think that United States' apathy and insensitivity

went unnoticed? Think again. The August 1939 issue of *Der Weltkampf* stated, "We are saying openly that we do not want the Jews, while the democracies keep on claiming that they are willing to receive them—and then leave the guests out in the cold! Aren't we savages better men after all?"

What is worse is that United States apathy served as a justification of Nazi policy. According to the *Danziger Vorposten*: "We see that one likes to pity the Jews as long as one can use this pity for a wicked agitation against Germany, but that no state is prepared to fight the cultural disgrace of Central Europe by accepting a few thousand Jews. This serves to justify Germany's policy against Jews."

You may be wondering why the United States did not want to admit refugees. I'll share some of the most popular excuses with you.

The Allies agreed that the dumping of large numbers of refugees would be dangerous, as some of these refugees might be spies in disguise. Tell me, how many of the thousands of small children who died in mass graves and gas chambers, just how many do you think were spies?

Some opponents of immigration said that in the aftermath of the Great Depression, refugees would be stealing jobs that rightfully belonged to unemployed American workers. Did any of these people ever stop to consider that these refugees would be consumers as well as workers and thus would provide as many jobs as they would take? Even so, is money more sacred than human life? How many dollars is one life worth anyway? What about six million lives?

Did the United States government really have a clear picture of what was happening in Europe? By August of 1942, Hitler had killed over one and a half million Jews. That month Dr. Stephen Wise brought detailed reports to the United States State Department describing Hitler's Final Solution. The reports were not verified and accepted as true until the following

November. In December, the Allies issued a declaration stating that after the war, the Nazis would be punished for the crimes they have committed against the Jews. In other words, the Allies were going to watch Hitler kill all the Jews and then when he was finished, then they were going to punish Germany.

Here is another interesting fact. The Allies knew exactly where the concentration camps and extermination camps were. Still, in 1944 the United States War Department rejected appeals to bomb the Auschwitz gas chambers and the railroads leading to Auschwitz. The reasons that they gave were that such an operation would "divert essential airpower from decisive operations elsewhere." They claimed that they would only bomb "military targets." Yet while these excuses were being made, the Americans were bombing areas not fifty miles from Auschwitz, and industrial targets within Auschwitz, not five miles from the gas chambers.

How could the American public allow their government to carry on this way? For some, a major reason was due to poor media coverage. Others simply did not care to know. The *New York Times* covered extermination related stories during late November and December of 1942, but except for one front page story on the United Nations declaration I discussed earlier, most of the news was hidden in between the pages. Yet, the *New York Times* provided by far the most complete American press coverage of Holocaust events. Take note of some important connections: Without adequate press, it became difficult to arouse public interest and indignation; this handicapped efforts to build grassroots pressure for government action to aid the Jews.

Stringent immigration policies went unchangeed and rescue proposals were ignored. The lack of public information made the United States and the Allied powers accomplices to Hitler in the crimes committed against the Jewish people during the Holocaust of World War II.

So what is left for us to do? We cannot resurrect six million lives. We cannot reunite millions of destroyed families. And, try as we might, we cannot turn back the hands of time. But there are a few things we can do. We can face the world with our eyes open, and never allow ourselves to become accomplices to apathy again. The homeless on our own streets have problems that desperately need our attention. There are elderly who need our care. Let us vow to understand what is happening in the world around us, but more importantly, let us make it our duty, our moral responsibility, to watch over our fellow man.

I leave you with a quote from a pastor named Martin Niemoeller:

> First they came for the Communists, and I did not speak out because I was not a Communist. Next they came for the Socialists, and I did not speak out because I was not a Socialist. Then they came for the trade unionists, and I did not speak out because I was not a trade unionist. Then they came for the Jews and I did not speak out because I was not a Jew. Then they came for me—and there was no one left to speak out for me.

—BR

7

Keep the Memory
of the Holocaust Alive
A Child of Survivors Speaks Out

I personally feel no guilt for having the God-given privilege of being alive. I mourn for my grandparents, uncles and aunts who perished at the hands of Nazi maniacs, often weeping for not having experienced their love. I cry in anguish when reminded that six million of my brethren, young and old, left this earth via gas chambers and crematoriums. I sense the pain of my family and friends who saw their elders shot before their very eyes and their babies hurled against brick walls and bayoneted. I experienced deep anger when I viewed the numbers branded on the arm of my father, of blessed memory. Yet I thanked God for sparing the lives of my beloved parents.

Yes, I blame humanity for remaining silent while my innocent brethren perished, screaming in terror for someone to heed their outcries. Humanity, not God. We are not puppets to be controlled by our creator. People caused the Holocaust; people remained silent. Leaders of countries refused to intercede on behalf of the defenseless.

Should I hate humanity? Should I live with anger in my heart, rebelling against the environment, rejecting those of other faiths and cultures? Perhaps I should bend in fear like a blade of grass when the winds of anti-semitism turn toward me. Perhaps I should walk along the rocky paths of a society that breeds hatred, fearing what the future may bring.

I openly and candidly answer in the negative. No, I will not live in a shell of neurotic chaos, and I will not reject society. I refuse to live in a world that rejects hope. I reject a world that is receiving nourishment from the seeds of hatred.

I admire and respect my beloved parents, Jacob and Rachel, of blessed memory, and honor them for their strength and courage. Even Auschwitz could not diminish their faith. They could have rejected humanity; instead they aided others in their daily fight for existence. No, a world of anger and hostility was not their banner.

Now that I am an orphaned adult, I appreciate even more the impact that my parents had upon me. All that I am and all that I ever will be I owe to them. They instilled within me pride and fortitude; their motto because my personal outcry, "Never again."

Refuse to discuss the Holocaust? Sweep these memories under the rug? No, this is not our mission to the world and ourselves. Let the truth be known! Let others realize what the world did to an ethical, moral and religious populace. Let them hear the testimony of valiant survivors. Let them see our courage.

Feel guilt for surviving, for speaking on behalf of children who were silenced—never!

I became a rabbi to aid the living, to ensure our survival, to rekindle the Jewish flame. I am proud; proud of my heritage, proud of our strength, and proud of my beloved parents.

Contrary to what we are told, the passage of time does not ease the pain, nor does it diminish the scope of the horror that was the Holocaust.

Oh yes, there are those, few in numbers, who feel that it is psychologically healthier to avoid reminders that keep painful and unpleasant events alive. Why subject our young to the brutal story of Nazi bestiality toward the Jewish people? What purpose will it serve? It would be wiser not to talk about it, so that it can disappear.

Never! We must never stop telling this story. Tell it we must, in every gory detail! We must do this because it is our sacred duty to alert the people to the evils of men, so that they will never be lulled into a false sense of safety and security. We must alert them so that our children will be vigilant and will never be caught unaware, as were the Jews who perished in the Holocaust. This is the message I emphasize to my beloved children, Ilana, Ayelet, Yaakov and Ari.

Although we are cognizant that our children will be adversely affected, that they will feel great pain upon learning the true facts of the Holocaust, we know that is something we must do.

I urgently beg of you, my fellow children of Holocaust survivors, keep alive the memory of the courage and will to live possessed by your parents. Time is growing short. Soon, like my parents of blessed memory, they will have left this world. Speak with them now. Learn all you can about their Holocaust experiences and about your grandparents and great-grandparents. Communicate with them before it is too late! This is our mission. This we must vow to do. Join me, my fellow Holocaust brothers and sisters, in this holy mission. Let us join hands and loudly acclaim, "We will keep the memory of the Holocaust alive."

—BR

8

Dignity and Resistance

I find it to be very painful and humiliating, as well as a perversion of the truth and reality, to hear people say that the Jews of the *Shoah* went to their death like sheep to the slaughter. This is one of the most insulting and humiliating statements hurled at the martyrs of the *Shoah*. It is an epithet that insults the good name and memory of those who died a saintly death.

It hurts me to hear people talk like that for many reasons. It hurts me because it insults the memory of my mother and father and infant brother who perished in the *Shoah*. They did not go like sheep to the slaughter. They went with dignity! They went under the guard of overwhelming numbers of soldiers,

Germans, Poles, Lithuanians, Ukrainians, Bialorussians, Estonians and Latvians alike. They did not go like sheep. They walked like human beings!

My six-month-old baby brother is not to be compared to a sheep. He had the imprint of God upon him. He was a martyr because he died as a Jew and because he was born a Jew.

My mother did not die like a sheep. She went to her death with dignity. She went to her death with tears flowing down her cheeks. She walked her last step with a prayer on her lips and faith in her heart, holding her infant son in her arms.

My father was not killed because he walked to the slaughter like a sheep. He was killed because he was a Jew. Though I was not present when he was killed, I know that he died the death of a martyr with the words *Shemah Israel* on his last breath.

I am hurt because the millions of Jews who perished in the *Shoah* did not die like sheep. They died a martyr's death!

It pains me when I hear people saying that the Jews died like sheep because but for the grace of God there go I. I hate to think of myself as having died as a sheep. I remember well sitting in the ditch by the roadside and waiting my turn to be taken to be shot, and now to be spoken of as having been killed like a sheep! Is this what it would have meant for me to have died as a Jew?

What does it mean to die like a sheep or to be led to the slaughter like sheep?

Presumably it means to allow oneself to be killed without offering any resistance, and to allow oneself to be killed when one had a chance to fight back and live, or, at least, to die fighting. It also assumes the corollary that to die fighting is ipso facto a virtue, and that to die without fighting for one's life is a vice. It implies that physical resistance is always the right thing to do. The Jews of the *Shoah*, then, are to stand accused of being guilty of all the above. What an outrage! What a shame! What a disgrace! What a scandal! What an obscenity! What a profanation of the sanctity of our noblest and holy martyrs!

It is a lie that the Jews of the *Shoah* did not offer any resistance to their murderers. They did not allow themselves to be led like sheep to the slaughter. They resisted and they fought back whenever and wherever they could. They fought back in the ghettos and in the concentration camps; in the partisans and in the cities; in the towns and in the villages. They fought back with their bare hands and with guns. They fought back as individuals and as organized military groups. They fought back, young and old; men and women. They fought back by running away to hide in the forests or amongst friends, rare as they were, and by standing defiantly to face death. They fought back with the guns and rifles and bullets that they bought from peasants and other non-Jews in exchange for the suits on their backs, the last few zlotys or rubles in their pockets. They fought with molotov cocktails and improvised mines. They fought with the weapons taken from their dead enemies. They fought back most of all by retaining their dignity, humanity, and their Jewishness, and by refusing to succumb and stoop to the despicable sub-humanity of their murderers. They did all of these things whenever they had a chance to do it. Alas, they did not always have the chance or the means to fight back. The Jews under the German occupation did not have to resist the Germans alone. That, if only that were all there was to do, might have been easy. The Jews unfortunately also had to fight and hide from their Polish, Russian, Ukrainian, Lithuanian, Estonian, Latvian, Bialorussian, French, Belgian and the other neighbors around them. There is not an insurrection movement in all human history that had to fight such a battle. All national resistance movements had some sort of support to fall back on in the midst of the indigenous population where they lived. The Jews alone among the nations had no such support. On the contrary, the indigenous populations themselves turned against the Jews and anyone of their kind who would dare to help them. The Jews thus did not only have to fight the Germans and their collaborators, but all the people around them, because they all joined hands with the Germans to kill the Jews. (That does not include the few noble and wonderful souls who risked, and often paid with, their lives in order to save a Jew. The paucity of such numbers only proves the point, if proof is needed). The Jews did not resist as those who sit in judgment of them after the *Shoah* would have wanted them to do, because they were overcome by immeasurably larger and merciless numbers. When and where they did have a chance, they fought gallantly and heroically, and they died fighting. I bear witness to this. In my own home town of Zshettel (Diatlova), our young and not so young men and women organized, and resisted the Germans. They fought back and died fighting. I remember when we were sitting in the ditch at the side of the road waiting to be shot how two young boys, mere teenagers, jumped up and started running away into the field, toward the nearby tiny forest, with the hope of escaping death. They ran no more than about five hundred feet before they were shot by a volley of gunfire coming from the rifles of the Wehrmacht soldiers who were guarding us and leading us to be killed. I remember many more acts of Jewish heroism, but this shall be enough for the moment.

Physical resistance is not the only form of resistance. It should not be assumed for a moment that just because Jews did resist and fight back during the *Shoah*, that physical force and resistance even as a last resort is automatically in and of itself a virtue. Indeed there are times when non-resistance is a greater virtue, and it alone becomes the only virtuous and heroic path to follow.

When one is inevitably going to die; when to fight means merely to die killing another life (even though it be that of a worthless creature), when to fight means to become like the enemy one fights and wants to kill; when to fight means to lose one's sense of pride, dignity and all that one stands for as a human being created in the image of God; when to fight means to become a brute and an animal like the murderer one confronts; when the odds of surviving a fight are zero; when all of these facts coincide, then physical resistance is not a virtue. It is not a virtue to die by turning into your enemy's likeness. On the contrary, at such a moment in time, it becomes a virtue not to die like him, but to chose such a way of dying that in death itself, one rises to the level of true humanity and so preserves the image of God in which we were all created. Thus, when the whole intention of one's enemy is to reduce one to the level of a beast, and to deprive one of any semblance of being a person created in the image of God, the best and most noble way to resist one's oppressors is to retain one's humanity and dignity to the very last moment of one's life. Thus, to walk to one's death with dignity, nay, and even with pride, is indeed the greatest form of resistance, and the ultimate victory of the victim over the murderer.

The Jews of the *Shoah* have displayed the highest form of resistance possible. They marched to their death with songs of hope in the coming of the Messiah and the redemption of the entire world. They went to the crematoriums with prayers on their lips. They were shot to death uttering their professions of faith in God. By their actions the Jews of the *Shoah* have denied and deprived their enemy of the very goal of all his actions—to dehumanize them. They have shown us the highest form of human resistance. They retained their human dignity and the Divine image in which they were created to the very end of their lives. Their souls returned to their heavenly abode untarnished by the brutality of their murderers. They did not go like sheep to the slaughter. They went like heroic angels returning to their eternal resting place.

—*CR*

9

The Sanctification
of God's Name

The immediate post-Holocaust generation has produced a
deluge of literature questioning the presence of God during
the dark days of the Holocaust. Some of these writings were
simple cries of pain at the absence of God. Others were sheer
expressions of atheistic exploitation of the singed hearts and
minds of the survivors. Still others were manifestations of the
beliefs of those people who were looking for an opportunity to
justify their anti-religious feeling and thinking. There is no doubt
that many good God fearing people could not cope with the fact
that God stood by and allowed the slaughter of millions of
innocent human beings without some intervention, and there-

fore they turned away from God, and in the hour of despair and disillusionment questioned God's goodness and concern for His creations. Indeed, some people turned against God. But that is not the whole picture nor the complete story.

Just as following the Holocaust there were people who turned against God because of what happened, there were also those who did not. Not all Holocaust Jews lost faith in God and proclaimed, "There is no law and there is no judge." There were also those people who did not waiver in their faith. Indeed even those people, and there were many, who did lose their faith in God, did so gradually and almost inadvertently; they succumbed little by little to the unceasing and torturous flow of events brought about by the murderous oppressors who not only deprived them of their humanity, but also their will and physical ability to live. As a result of this, people just slid out of their religious faith and were swept away by the tide of cruelty and evil that flooded the world, never to return. Yet in spite of this, miraculously, many people remained true to the faith of their fathers and even went so far as to sanctify God's name both with their lives and their death.

The Talmud,[1] commenting on the passage from the Torah,

> The Rock, His work is perfect;
> For all His ways are justice;
> A God of faithfulness and without iniquity,
> Just and right is He.[2]

tells us the following story while at the same time teaching us how to interpret this beautiful passage of the Torah.

When the Romans led Rabbi Chanina, the son of Tradion,

---

[1] *Avodah Zarah* 18a.
[2] Deuteronomy 32:4.

---

his wife and daughter to be burned at the stake, they justified God's law as it applied to them.

He said: "The Rock His work is perfect for all His ways are justice." His wife said: "A God of faithfulness without iniquity just and right is He." His daughter said: "Great in council and mighty in work; Whose eyes are open upon all the ways of the sons of men, To give every one according to the fruit of his doings."[3]

Who would dare count how many Rabbi Chaninas there were in the Holocaust? Who would dare count how many wives like Rabbi Chanina's wife there were in those dark days? And who would dare count the number of daughters who like Rabbi Chanina's daughter sanctified God's name with their last breath?

There are endless stories of Jewish Holocaust martyrs going to their death singing:

> *Ahnee Ma'amin Be'Emunah Shlaymah*
> *B'vi'at Ha'Mashi'ach*
> *V'af Al Pi She'Yitma'me'ah*
> *B'chol Zot Achakeh Loh B'chol Yom She'Yavoh*

(I believe with a perfect faith in the coming of the Messiah and even though he may tarry, I will in spite of this await his coming everyday.)

There are also many, many stories of people who refused to run away and instead walked with dignity to their deaths. I remember how I watched, with the bewilderment that only a child of six years of age can feel, men, women and children, young and old alike, being led in groups of ten or twelve to be shot. I remember how the reverberation of the noise of the volleys of the firearms would come to us from just inside the

---

[3]Jeremiah 32:19.

51

woods in front of which we were sitting and waiting for our turn to come, and all I could hear and see around me were people praying and crying, and indeed not so much crying as praying in a language that I could not understand. I remember how people tried to move to the back of the line in the hope that their turn to die would be delayed, or by some miracle that they would be saved if only they could postpone their turn to go to death by a few minutes.

I also remember how other people did not budge from their place, and when their turn came to go, they stood up and walked with dignity and in silence to return their souls to their Maker.

I remember the story of Dr. Winick in my hometown who refused to be separated from his sister, and be saved. Instead, he went together with her to their death. I remember that the first thing we, who survived the slaughter of our town, did when we met in the forest for the first time was to organize a Minyan in order to *daven*—pray—the afternoon and evening service and say kaddish. The only problem that was encountered was to find someone who knew the services by heart. There was a father and two sons who did know, and so services were conducted and all men participated. I do not recall anyone objecting or questioning God at that time.

I also remember years later my teacher, Rabbi Abraham Kravetz, of blessed memory, tell, one Sabbath afternoon as we were sitting in the warmth of his home enjoying the delight of a Sabbath afternoon discussion, that during the war he lost all willpower to struggle in order to survive. Had it not been for his wife, who urged him on to make every effort to live, he would not have survived. When I asked him why, he replied, "Because there is a principle in the Talmud that states, 'One must follow the majority,' and since almost everybody was being killed, I felt that I should also follow the majority, for this must be God's will. Therefore I should not oppose that which God has ordained."

And so he concluded he did not want to go against God's will by going out of his way to save himself.

The stories of the martyrdom of the Jewish sons and daughters, the wives and husbands, the rabbis and scholars who went on their last journey on this earth as they entered Heaven with dignity and pride, unfathomable faith and fidelity to their God and the God of their fathers, cannot be counted any more than the stars of the heavens can be. Can anyone imagine how many times *Shma Israel*—"Hear O Israel the Lord Our God, the Lord is One" was uttered? With each agonizing and tortured last breath that was gasped in pain as the souls of our martyrs left their mortal abodes and went up to heaven through the chimneys of the concentrations camps, from the mass graves of the ghettos, from the bunkers and caves in the forest and swamps of Belarus, Ukraine and Poland, from the burned, shot, beaten to death, starved and frozen bodies of our saintly sons, daughters, mothers and fathers all over Europe, God's law was justified! Each one of them proclaimed with his and her last breath, "Blessed be the righteous judge!" They, by their actions, taught us that they accepted God's will for better or for worse. In doing this they lived up to the teaching of our sages that we must bless God equally for the good and for the bad things in life that happen to us. They accepted it because they regarded it as God's will and looked upon themselves as God's servants whose duty it was to do God's bidding. Ralph Waldo Emerson said, "The ways of Providence are incalculable. It is often wild and rough . . . and it is of no use to try to whitewash its huge, mixed instrumentalities." Our martyrs did not "try to whitewash" these "huge, mixed instrumentalities." Indeed, none could be more huge and wild than the "instrumentalities" of the Holocaust. But our holy martyrs did not try to explain them away! They accepted them! They lived with them! They died with them!

Unfortunately these facts are hardly mentioned in the secular literature of the Holocaust that has become the currency of Holocaust studies and popular culture of our time. Only in the Yiddish and in some Hebrew literature about the Holocaust can these facts be found. Until they are brought out into the light and included in the popularized literature of the Holocaust, the memory of our martyrs will not be served, and their legacy of martyrdom will not be immortalized.

—*CR*

10

Hitler Speaks

In *Mein Kamp*, Hitler repeatedly insisted on the power of the spoken word. This maniac hypnotized the masses by believing the following: "I know that one is able to win people far more by the spoken, than by the written word, and that every great movement on this globe owes its rise to the great speakers and not to the great writers."[1]

This strange, daemonic man meant every word he uttered. "There shall be no privation in Germany which I myself do not also accept," Hitler said. "My whole life belongs to my people

---

[1] Peterson and Houston, ed. *A Treasury of the World's Great Speeches* (New York: Simon and Schuster, 1965), p. 757.

from now on—in a new sense. I wish nothing other than to be the first soldier of the German Reich. I have therefore put on that tunic that once before was the dearest and most sacred to me, and I shall take it off after victory has been won—or I shall not live to experience the end."[2]

At the age of twenty, Hitler worked as a common laborer in the building trade. He found his fellow workmen uncongenial; they had reciprocal feelings. At first ready to aid him in acquiring mechanical skill, they soon learned to despise him due to his pretensions of belonging to a higher social level. "His political views bewildered them; his contempt for trade-unionism annoyed them. Above all, they were irked by the violent manner of his discussion, his lack of self-control, his intolerance of others' opinions, his fury at being contradicted. He could not bear debate; he demanded the place of sole orator. He would attempt to support his torrid arguments with references to some of his ill-digested reading."[3] Adolf read in a haphazard fashion. The only literature that held his attention was that which would support his nefarious prejudices.

Edgar Ansel Mowrer describes the inconsistencies of the German soul: "To the outside world Germany seems the country of organized science. But equally it is the country of rampant superstition. This people is rich in intellect, poor in common sense. It is a country where men are continually flying to extremes that meet again at the end of some unexpected rainbow."[4] The German may be described as a "Dr. Jekyll and Mr. Hyde." He is the product of opposing characteristics. He is a creature of constant *Sturm und Drang*, of storm and stress and

---

[2]Wallace R. Duel, *People Under Hitler* (New York: Harcourt Brace, 1942), p. 5.
[3]Morris D. Waldman, *Sieg Heil* (Dobbs Ferry, NY: Oceana Pub., 1962,) p. 12.
[4]Duel, p. 25.

---

striving, of self-consciousness and self-examination. Mowrer says, "Everything you say of such people must promptly be completed by its opposite."[5]

The German's respect for authority is proverbial. His respect for authority stems from the German's thirst for order and regulation in everything. The German always gets impressive results. The German might devote twice the time and effort necessary to gain results. The German's passion for order is ardent. Wallace R. Duel, author of *People Under Hitler*, claims that the German is unhappy unless and until everybody else is compelled to live the way he thinks he ought to. "The German does not accept discipline because of a neat love for order," Dorothy Thompson writes. "He accepts it the way a drunkard delivers himself into a sanitarium. He wants somebody to impose it on him because he cannot impose it on himself."[6]

The most comprehensive and far-reaching attempt to apply the psychoanalytical approach to the Hitler movement is that of Frederick L. Schuman, in his book *The Nazi Dictatorship*.

> "Fundamentally the psychic disorder was a disease of the *Kleinburgertum* (the lower middle class). This group suffered from acute paranoia, typical delusions of persecution and systematic hallucinations of grandeur. In Hitler it found at least an articulate voice. In the *Weltanschauung* of the Nazi party it found solace for all its woes, forgiveness for all sins, justification for all its hatreds, scapegoats for all its misfortunes, and a millennial vision of all its hopes."[7]

According to Schuman, the *Kleinburgertum* yearned for what was hard, well-armored, even brutal, to disguise and forget its

---

[5]Ibid., p. 27.
[6]Ibid., p. 34.
[7]Frederick L. Schuman, *The Nazi Dictatorship* (New York: Knopf, 1935), p. 109.

own weakness.[8] "The Germans possess a strong desire for militarism. The forbidden but sanctified pleasures of mass murder were too keenly relished. Death-fears and guilt-feelings were transmuted into a highly enjoyable cult of 'heroism' and admiration for that which has furnished opportunities for permissible sins and crimes."[9] "Anti-semitism was a pathological phenomenon, a persecution to appease the unconscious guilt feelings of the persecutors and to afford a convenient discharge for aggression in a direction relatively harmless to the established order."[10]

The stage has now been set. The audience has been analyzed. The motives have been established. All that is needed now is the "star" of this tragic world drama. That was his "ethos?" How could he manipulate the minds of seemingly intelligent people? Hitler served a dual function; he was chief executive and prophet of the movement. Adolf Hitler was the genius of the movement. He was a dauntless executive. This strong-willed leader possessed a keen sense for organization and a realistic sense for dealing with his associates. To the Germans, Hitler was "a prophet whose pronounce-ments were taken as oracles. In their eyes he was a hero whom they naively trusted to perform the impossible if necessary. He was endowed by them with that highest degree of prestige which emanates not merely from the recognition of one's own inability to imitate or compete with such a person, but from the belief that he possesses an out-of-the-ordinary, super-human power, that a special star is guiding his destiny."[11]

Hitler's past was representative of the masses; thus, an important feeling of empathy was created. The masses, once

---

[8]Ibid., p. 108.
[9]Ibid., p. 108.
[10]Ibid., p. 112.
[11]Theodore Abel, *The Why of the Hitler Movement* (New York: Prentice Hall, 1938), p. 181.

well-established in middle-class society, now were forced to the lowest level of the proletariat. So was Hitler. He supposedly served in a German army that was invincible. So had millions of others. Hitler needed an explanation for the catastrophes that had occurred. So did the masses. The explanation was forthcoming. According to Hitler, the true German people were the greatest of all the peoples on the earth. They were destined to rule the earth; however, they had allowed the enemies within the gates to betray them. It was all the fault of the Jews.

At this point, I feel it incumbent upon me to interject my own personal opinion. I cannot accept the previously given stereotypes as being valid in all cases. I am quite certain that many heroic and God fearing Germans perished in Stadelheim, Dachau, Buchenwald and elsewhere. Unfortunately, I must deal with generalities.

The searchlight of history now focuses upon the rhetorical abilities of Adolf Hitler. The following are parts of the speech that first disclosed his menacing intentions against Europe.[12] "Germany's Claims" was delivered on February 20, 1938:

> Despite the really exemplary discipline, strength and restraint which National Socialists preserved in their revolution, we have seen that a certain portion of the foreign press inundated the new Reich with a virtual flood of lies and calumnies. It was a remarkable mixture of arrogance and deplorable ignorance which led them to act as the judges of a people who should be presented as models of these democratic apostles.
>
> The best proof for showing up these lies is success. For if we had acted during these five years like the democratic

---

[12] Copeland and Lamb, ed. *The World's Great Speeches* (New York: Dover Pub., 1958), p. 474.

world citizens of Soviet Russia, that is, like those of the Jewish race, we would not have succeeded in making out of a Germany, which was in the deepest material collapse, a country of material order. For this very reason we claim the right to surround our work with that protection which renders it impossible for criminal elements or for the insane to disturb it. Whoever disturbs this mission is the enemy of the people, whether he pursues his aim as a Bolshevist democrat, a revolutionary terrorist or a reactionary dreamer. In such a time of necessity those who act in the name of God are not those who, citing Bible quotations, wander idly about the country and spend the day partly doing nothing and partly criticizing the work of others; but those whose prayers take the highest form of uniting man with his God, that is the form of work.

I had a right to turn against every one who, instead of helping, thought his mission was to criticize our work. Foreign nations contributed nothing apart from this spirit, for their rejection was tinged by hate or a spirit of knowing better than we know.

"German Conquests" delivered in May 1941: (Excerpts are presented.)

On May 10 of last year perhaps the most memorable struggle in all German history commenced. The enemy front was broken up in a few days and the stage was then set for the operation that culminated in the greatest battle of annihilation in the history of the world. Thus France collapsed, Belgium and Holland were already occupied, and the battered remnants of the British expeditionary force were driven from the European continent, leaving their arms behind.

On July 19, 1940, I then convened the German

Reichstag for the third time in order to render that great account which you all still remember. The meeting provided me with the opportunity for expressing the thanks of the nation to its soldiers in a form suited to the uniqueness of the event.

Once again I seized the opportunity of urging the world to make peace. And what I foresaw and prophesied at that time happened. My offer of peace was misconstrued as a symptom of fear and cowardice.

The European and American warmongers succeeded once again in befogging the common sense of the masses, who can never hope to profit from this war, by conjuring up false pictures of new hope. Thus, finally, under pressure of public opinion, as formed by their press, they once more managed to induce the nation to continue this struggle.[13]

In the words of Hjalmar Shacht, "Adolf played like a virtuoso on the well-tempered piano of lower middle class hearts." The following techniques frequently occur in Hitler's speeches. (They are evident in the previously presented rhetorical selections.) The speaker should always instill the masses with faith, not with knowledge. Faith moves mountains. The driving force behind revolutions has never been a body of scientific teaching, but a devotion that has inspired masses of people and an hysteria that has catapulted them into action. To win the masses one must have the key to their emotions; and where gentle persuasion will not turn the key one must exert one's will, and, if need be, support it by force. The lock and key are not a complicated mechanism—just a few stereotyped formulas, brief and to the point, for the crowd can absorb only small doses. These slogans must, however, be constantly repeated so that they will be

---

[13]Ibid., pp. 484–485.

indelibly impressed upon the mind, because the memory of the crowd is short.[14]

The spoken word is mightier than the pen. Every utterance must be passionate and fanatical; therefore, these same passions will infect the hearer with a renewed zest and loyalty. The hearer must always be flattered; their intelligence, integrity and above all their patriotism must be constantly praised. Simultaneously the vices of the enemy such as greed, cowardice and treachery must be highlighted.

By eliciting hatred from the audience and transferring their hatred to potential victims, audience manipulation is achieved. Moved by terror, decent men will commit every insidious crime, including mass murder. The "lie" should be extensively employed; however, when you lie make it a big lie; the very bigness of the lie will make it credible. The masses would not suspect one who dares utter such enlightening remarks.

Whenever accused, don't answer the charge, merely disparage the accuser. Paint the accuser as a wicked, malicious liar.

Hitler points out in *Mein Kampf*, "It soon became evident that our opponents when debating with us, were armed with a definite repertoire of arguments and that their points against our claims kept constantly recurring in their speeches; this similarity pointed to conscious and unified training. When I spoke, it was important to get a clear idea beforehand of the probable form and character of the arguments we had to expect during the discussion, and then tear them to pieces in my own opening speech; the thing was not to mention all the possible arguments (*contra*) at once and prove their hollowness."[15]

The orator, according to Hitler,

---

[14]Waldman, p. 43.
[15]Adolf Hitler, *My Battle*, E. T. S. Dugdale, trans. (Boston: Houghton Mifflin Co., 1955), p. 197.

receives continuous guidance from his audience, enabling him to correct his lecture, since he can measure all the time, on the countenances of his hearers, the extent to which they are successful in following his arguments intelligently and whether his words are producing the effect he desires, whereas the writer has no acquaintance with his readers. Hence he is unable to prepare his sentences with a view to addressing a definite crowd of people, sitting in front of his eyes, but he is obliged to argue in general terms.

Supposing that an orator observes that his hearers do not understand him, he will make his explanation so elementary and clear that every single one must take it in; if he feels that they are incapable of following him, he will build up his ideas carefully and slowly until the weakest member has caught up; again, when once he senses that they seem not to be convinced that he is correct in his argument, he will repeat then over and over again with fresh illustrations and himself state their unspoken objections; he will continue thus until the last group of the opposition show him by their behavior and play of expression that they have capitulated to his demonstration of the case.[16]

The hour of the day has a decided effect.

The same address delivered by the same speaker on the same subject has quite a different effect at ten o'clock in the morning from what it has at three in the afternoon or in the evening. . . . Fine oratory by a dominant apostolic character will be more successful in the evening in inducing men, whose powers of resistance are by that late hour sensibly weakened in the natural course, than men who are

---

[16]Ibid., p. 199.

in full possession of their energy of mind and volition. The same purpose is served by the artificially produced, mysterious dim light in Roman Catholic churches, the lighted candles, incense and censers.[17]

Mass assemblies are necessary because, while attending them, the individual who feels on the point of joining a young movement takes alarm if left by himself receives his first impression of a larger community, and this has a strengthening and encouraging effect on most people. He submits himself to a magic influence of what we call 'mass suggestion,'[18] and armed guards and vividly colored posters with the symbolic swastika surrounded by slogans encouraged group cohesiveness.

Otto Strasser, a Nazi leader who broke with Hitler and later fled the Terror, wrote,

Hitler responds to the vibration of the human heart with the delicacy of a seismograph, or perhaps of a wireless receiving set, enabling him, with a certainty with which no conscious gift could endow him, to act as a loudspeaker proclaiming the most secret desires, the least admissible instincts, the sufferings and personal revolts of a whole nation. . . . I have been asked many times what is the secret of Hitler's extraordinary power as a speaker. I can only attribute it to his uncanny intuition, which infallibly diagnoses the ills from which his audience is suffering. If he tries to bolster up his arguments with theories or quotations from books he has only imperfectly understood, he scarcely rises above a very poor mediocrity. But let him throw away his crutches

---

[17]Ibid., p. 200.
[18]Ibid., p. 202.

and step out boldly, speaking as the spirit moves him, and he is promptly transformed into one of the greatest speakers of the century. . . . Adolf Hitler enters a hall. He sniffs the air, For a minute he gropes, feels his way, senses the atmosphere. Suddenly he bursts forth. His words go like an arrow to their target, he touches each private wound on the raw, liberating the mass unconscious, expressing its innermost aspirations, telling it what it most wants to hear.[19]

And do this at the top of your voice; the louder you shriek, the more passionate your seemingly righteous outbursts are, the more you will convince the audience of your sincerity, therefore, empathy is achieved. The thick, harsh voice that can be so repellent plays its part in the spell that Hitler's oratory creates. Professor M. D. Steer of Purdue University has analyzed Hitler's voice and states that it is his high pitch and its accompanying emotion that put the people in a passive state; he stuns them with his words in much the same manner as we are stunned by an auto horn. In *Nazi Propaganda*, Zbynek A. B. Zeman writes, "Hitler's power as a speaker lay mainly in the rapport he established between himself and the audience. The opening moves of every speech he made were hesitant. The attitude of his body was stiff, he was feeling his way like a blind man; his voice was muted and monotonous. After a few minutes, this apparent unwillingness to communicate gave way to a steadier, louder flow of sentences; the speaker's muscles visibly relaxed, and he was soon to begin using his right arm in gestures that resembled blows aimed at an invisible nail. Then the flow increased into a torrent; the punch line was delivered in a loud, sometimes hoarse, high-pitched voice; the end was abrupt. A new paragraph, another train of thought, was then introduced in a softer voice though not in the

---

[19]Waldman, p. 43.

same halting manner as the opening of the speech; the clockwork was again seen by the spellbound audience to unwind itself, the crescendo was once more achieved, and wiped out by a wide sweep of the right arm. The onslaught on the eardrums of the audience was tremendous: It was estimated that the frequency of Hitler's voice in a typical sentence was 228 vibrations per second, whereas 200 vibrations is the usual frequency of a voice raised in anger."[20]

Adolf Hitler is dead; his spirit lingers on in other demonic bodies. If genocide is to be prevented in the future, we must understand how it happened in the past. We can no longer be bystanders to cruelty; if we are, we become bystanders to genocide.

The fantastic scene in the elaborate catacombs below the streets of Berlin, confirmed the eternal truth of the Hebrew prophet Zechariah: "Not by might, nor by power, but by my spirit, saith the Lord of Hosts."

—BR

[20]Zybnek A. B. Zeman, *Nazi Propaganda* (London: Oxford University Press, 1964), p. 11.

11

Don't Wait Too Long to Appreciate Your Parents

Three years old—My daddy and mommy can do anything.

Five years old—My daddy and mommy are really smart.

Six years old—My daddy and mommy are smarter than yours.

Eight years old—My daddy and mommy know everything.

Nine years old—In the ancient days when my parents grew up, things were very, very different.

Eleven years old—My parents are eighty years old. They don't remember being children.

Thirteen years old—Don't pay any attention to my parents. They are simply old-fashioned. They belong in the Dark Ages.

Twenty-one years old—Who can cope with them? They are totally out of touch with reality.

Twenty-eight years old—Maybe I should call my parents. They do have more experience than I do.

Thirty-five years old—Am I glad I spoke to my parents. I could have really messed this one up.

Forty years old—I wish dad was alive. I need his business advice.

Forty-five years old—I wonder how my parents would have handled it. How in the world did they cope? I feel as if the world is caving in on me. They must have been superhuman. I would give anything if I could only talk to them once again. Too bad I didn't realize how smart they were. I could have learned so much more from them. I hope my children will be smarter than I was.

NOTE: This was written in memory of my parents, Jacob and Rachel Rosenberg, of blessed memory, survivors of the Holocaust.

—BR

12

Letter from a Child to Mom and Dad

(Written by a child of Holocaust survivors)

Dear Mom and Dad,

It is hard for me to say these things directly to you. Please read this letter. Don't be angry. I write these thoughts because I love you and I know you care and love me.

Spoiling me is not a good idea. I really do know that I shouldn't have everything I scream for. Trust me. I'm testing you.

When you are firm with me I know you care. In fact, it makes me feel more secure.

If you see me forming bad habits, please tell me. I need you to detect them while I am young.

When you make me feel smaller than I am, it only makes me behave stupidly big. Treat me with respect.

When you correct me in front of others, I am embarrassed. Speak to me quietly in private.

You know sometimes I say "I hate you." Believe me, I don't hate you. I am afraid of your power.

Nagging, being overly protective, making a mountain out of a molehill over childish mistakes, these are all "no no's." Remember, you were once a child too.

Sometimes I have problems explaining myself. Remember, I can't speak as well as you do.

Answer me when I ask you questions. Don't put off giving me an answer until you have time.

Please be consistent. I become confused and begin to doubt you otherwise.

Never tell me that my fears are silly. They are real to me.

I hate it when you tell me you are a grown up and know better. Sometimes you also make mistakes, and then I am really confused.

There is nothing wrong in saying that you were wrong. An apology goes a long way. It makes me love you even more.

I love to experiment. It's part of being a child. Don't you remember?

Growing up is not easy. Never forget that.

I need you, Mom and Dad. Please give me a lot of love. Please understand me. Remember, I love and need you.

Love, your child . . .

—*BR*

13

We Don't Want Your Medicine

Sticks and stones may break my bones, but names will never hurt me. Call me this, call me that, call yourself a dirty rat. Khalid Abdul Muhammad delivered an inane insulting diatribe against innocent Jews, resulting in his receiving a slightly tainted academy award from the Farrakhanites. Years ago this award called "Dumbo" was first invented by a liar named Adolf Hitler. The purpose of this award was to honor those who could invent the biggest outlandish lies. The ingredients for creating such a lie consisted of one percent truth and ninety-ninte percent fabrication. The bigger the lie, the better. After all, who took Adolf Hitler seriously in the 1920's? He looked like Charlie Chaplin, wiggled his mustache, and years later six million Jews were massacred.

What's the fuss? So he made a few stupid remarks. After all, only morons with an intelligence level of two would believe the trash regurgitated by such a peon of virtue. Who would believe that someone named Goldstein actually rules the gold market? By the way, someone should tell Dr. Muhammad that Goldstein is of German origin. Since my last name is Rosenberg, I must presume that my ancestors ruled mountains of roses.

Dr. Muhammad plays an interesting chess game. He tries to outwit his opponents by confusing the truth with fabricated historical distortions. Truth is mixed with absolute lies. Half truths leave the listener with distorted impressions. The Farra-khans and Muhammads hide behind free speech. However, it must be noted that hate speech is not part of legitimate debate. At best, hate speech is pornographic in nature and should be controlled.

Farrakhan and Muhammed utilize such infamous tactics as distorting the work of Jewish scholars and religious Jewish literature. Farrakhan declares that "seventy-five percent of the slaves owned in the South were owned by Jewish slave holders." It is interesting to note that in 1860, there were approximately 15,000 Southern Jews and four million slaves. According to Farrakhan's brilliant remarks, this would mean that every Jewish household owned 1,000 slaves. How ludicrous! If you want to blame someone, blame the Arabs who were the leaders in slave trade.

There is enough blame to go around in this world. It is wrong to hate Jews. It is also equally wrong to hate blacks, homosexuals, women, Catholics, and whites.

Sticks and stones may break my bones, but names will never hurt me. So why am I getting so excited? History has taught us that verbal lies can kill. Were it not for the vicious lies of Hitler and his band of Nazi maniacs, six million of my brethren might still be alive. Because of "names," my parents lost their youth in concentration camps. Because of "names," I do not have grandparents, aunts, or uncles. They vanished in the smoke stacks of Auschwitz. Because of "names," I grew up viewing the numbers that were branded on my father's arm. These "names" really did hurt me. Call me this, call me that, call yourself a dirty rat. Dr. Farrakhan and Dr. Muhammed, you may be doctors of the big lie, but I want no part of your medicine. I do not seek nor do I want your approval for my existence. We Jews have survived the crusades, the Pharaohs of Egypt, and the Hitlers. We will continue to survive with or without your blessing.

—BR

14

Bigotry and Hatred Still Exist

What a dumb blonde! Blonde bombshell! Another dizzy blonde! Blondes have more fun. These stereotypes have more truth to them than you would think. In a study conducted at random colleges across the nation, blondes' average SAT score is eighty points lower than brunettes'. Brunettes also have a higher acceptance rate to law school and medical school. In a survey by insurance companies, blondes are involved in twenty-two percent more accidents than non-blondes.

In the Miss USA Pageant, which stresses beauty and poise, blondes have won seven out of the past ten years. In the Miss

America Pageant, which places more emphasis on scholarship and talent, blondes have only won in two out of the last ten years.

These statistics are enlightening. They are especially interesting when you take into consideration that they are all lies. Complete and utter lies. They were created to demonstrate how simple it is to believe statements that impact on existing stereotypes. People begin by innocently believing rumors and fallacies. The end result is bigotry and hatred.

Minorities are often the victims of these misrepresentations. They are blamed for creating economic misfortune, undermining nations, and destroying social values.

This hatred is indiscriminate. No one should feel safe. All of us, in one way or another, may feel the sting of being part of a minority. Whether it be race, religion, gender, nationality, economic standing, profession, social group or political alliance, someone might hate you for just being alive. How can we allow such bigotry? What choice do we have? Is there anything we can do?

One of the most well-known incidents in recent history of hatred bred by propaganda and distorted information was the Holocaust. It is important to remember that not only were the Jews persecuted, but also others who did not conform to the Aryan image. *Aryan* is a term used by the Nazis to describe a non-Jewish Caucasian of Nordic extraction.

Anti-semitism was rampant in Europe, especially in Germany. Jews were depicted as the evil, power-hungry demons who were destroying Germany. The Germans were despondent. They were searching for a scapegoat. The German society was saturated with lies and misconceptions; soon the populace accepted these lies as facts. Six million Jews—men, women and children—were brutally murdered, for one and only one reason: they were Jews.

Anti-semitism still exists. A new world order is emerging in Europe and Russia. Once again, distorted images of Jews have arisen. In addition to anti-semitism, there now exists a blatant hatred against foreigners. Recently, the highest number of racially motivated attacks since the early Nazi era was recorded in Germany. German police stood quietly by as four Africans were attacked by men with baseball bats and chains—one of the Africans was killed. Neo-Nazis recently attacked a building housing children from the Chernobyl area who were sent there by their parents to protect them from the radioactive fallout.

Anti-Semites are raising their ugly heads throughout Europe. In Italy, ten and a half percent of the population feels that the Jews should leave their country. In Hungary, the term *Jewish* used as a slur, now means "traitor." A Hungarian soccer team originally founded by Jews over one hundred years ago now hears fans chant, "No goals for the Jews. Dirty Jews. Jews. Jews. To the gas chambers, gas chambers." Ironically, the team now consists entirely of non-Jews.

America is not exempt from anti-semitism. Anti-semitism is still widespread. In a study conducted by the Anti-Defamation League of over forty million Americans, one in five were shown to be anti-semitic.

In Germany over one quarter of the population feels that the Jews were at least partially at fault for the way they were treated. Jewish women were raped by soldiers in front of their husbands—babies were torn away from their mothers and shot—men, women and children were murdered in gas chambers and crematoriums. Human beings were starved to death while demonic Nazis conducted diabolical medical experiments upon innocent victims. How is it possible for any German in 1997 to believe that Jews deserved such inhuman treatment?

It is incumbent upon all of humanity to fight prejudice wherever it may exist. We must fight back. An attack upon one minority is an attack against all minorities. We must demonstrate an active resistance instead of passive acceptance.

—*BR*

15

The New York and *London Times* on Nazism (1933–39)

The beatings, torture, riots and anti-semitic legislation all occurred. In the pre-war years 1933–39, how much of it was reported? What did the American and English public know about the cruelty of the Nazi state toward it Jewish citizens? Despite the daily reports of murder, beatings and torture in the name of the Nazi Party led by Hitler, *The New York* and *London Times* reporters subscribed to the myth of Hitler as a man above politics. Hitler at the beginning was portrayed as the leader of an industrialized modern state, and not as the demonic force behind violence.

Where were the editorials asking for action to help the

tormented Jews? Where were the outcries for help? As the reader will see, the press was relatively silent.

On January 30, 1933, Hitler finally achieved political power as Chancellor of Germany. It was the first important step in his relentless campaign outlined so clearly in his *Mein Kampf.* On January 31, *The New York Times*, in a page three story entitled "Hitler Puts Aside Aim to be Dictator," reports that the coalition compromise that resulted in Hitler's ascent would most likely prove to bring an over-all "calm" upon German politics. It also stated that there should be little fear of Hitler's pre-stated ambitions. In an editorial on page sixteen, the editors expressed their contention that Hitler would never assume dictatorial status because of the peculiar political balance of German labor with their threats of strikes, because of the "strong and conservative hands" in which the national finances are kept, and mostly because President Hindenburg will retain "supreme command" and would be prepared to "unmake Hitler as quickly as he has made him." It also states: "Much of his old editorial thunder has either been stolen from him or has died down into a negligible rumble. The more violent parts of his alleged program he has himself in recent months been softening down or abandoning."

The London Times of January 31, 1933, carries a similar story. On page nine, in a story entitled "The New German Cabinet," *The London Times* states that "there is little of the alarm such an event would have provoked a short time ago . . . it is certainly not he [President von Hindenburg] that has given way." In summation, the article states that "added to all the caution which the situation demands, there is the hope that Hitler in power may prove less dangerous that a Hitler unhampered by responsibility." It is interesting to note that neither in *The London Times* nor in *The New York Times* is there any mention of Hitler's anti-semitic rhetoric.

During the week of March 11, 1933, the world received its first taste of Nazi zeal. In Braunschweig and Breslau, Jewish-owned department stores were forcibly closed and some destroyed. Storm troopers ejected Jewish judges and lawyers from the courts. Also, Dr. Jacob Listschinsky, the Berlin correspondent of the *Jewish Daily Forward*, was arrested by the police for collecting extracts from the Nazi press from which he concluded that a pogrom was about to occur. In a March 12 editorial (page 4 of section 40) *The New York Times* properly observed: "Foremost among the victorious Nazi and Nationalist slogans has been the call to repudiate the shame of the last fifteen years, to return to the Germany that was before 1918. It is going back sheer to the Dark Ages, and an ugly complex of ignorance, superstition, fear and hate."

This response by the press can conceivably be associated with the novelty of the situation. Never in modern times has a nation that prides itself on its order and on its cultural development lowered itself to such primitive levels. Unfortunately, however, the novelty began to wear off.

In response to the work of World Jewry, in their raising the voices of world opinion against Nazi policy, the National Socialist Party declared a boycott to begin on April 1, 1933, of all Jewish businesses in Germany. Dr. Goebbels, the German Minister for Propaganda, announced on March 31, that the boycott would end at 10:00 PM on Saturday, April 1, and then would continue with "full rigor" on Wednesday, April 5, unless the "atrocity campaign" of the foreign press ceased. The press's reaction to this event is indeed very interesting. In *The New York Times* of April 1, on a front page story entitled "Nazis Cut Boycott Today with Threat of Renewal if World Does Not Recant," comments:

> The outstanding fact in all this, however, is that the boycott has been whittled to a nine-hour demonstration tomorrow with renewed threats as to what may happen later. One would like to believe this to be a last-hour concession to the sober remonstrances of the few thinking Germans there

seem to be left in the maelstrom of ultranationalistic frenzy. Instead, it must be confessed that the movement has been revealed rather as a gigantic bluff and as a triumph of propaganda on a scale never before achieved here, even in wartime.

The New York Times refused to consider the sincerity of Nazi zeal and dismissed the boycott as an innocent tool of Nazi propaganda. On page 14 of its April 3, 1933, edition, *The London Times* reported the following:

> The attitude of the public towards the extraordinary scenes of yesterday seemed to be mainly passive. There is among the masses little spontaneous and active anti-semitism, though there is a widespread feeling of dislike and mistrust of certain alleged characteristics of a community which, as yesterday's events vividly showed, greatly predominates in business life, while forming less than one per cent of the population. . . . There is no spontaneous hostility to the hard-working small Jewish shopkeeper or trader.

The New York Times observed: "There has been nothing spontaneous about this boycott any more than there is any active anti-semitism in the German masses if they are left alone."[1] "Un-German Books Destroyed" was the title of a small and easily missed page 13 story in *The London Times* of May 11, 1933. It briefly reported the widespread and well-organized burnings of books considered offensive to the Nazi ethic. Almost no mention was made of the anti-semitic nature of this event. The same can be said of a similar article of the same date (page 16) appearing in the *New York Times*. The *New York Times* referred to this action as nothing more than a "school-boyish act."

---

[1] *The New York Times*, April 1, 1933, p. 1.

The two years following the book burnings were not years of serenity for German Jews. Nonetheless, they were able to go about their lives with relative normality. Then the Nuremberg Laws of September 15, 1935, were put into effect. Whatever doubts still remained as to the peril and survival of German Jewry should have been dismissed. The Jew was henceforth legally removed from the mainstream of German life. The swastika was now the official flag of the German peoples. The Jews could no longer marry or engage in "illicit relations" with Aryans. They could no longer retain German girls for domestic help in their homes. And they could no longer be citizens.[2] The *New York Times* still retained its optimism: "All this is innocently explained as going back to the methods of the Middle Ages. But civilization will not long be content to march backward in that way. The reason given by Hitler is frankly a pagan reason. This is one more proof that it cannot prevail for any length of time."[3]

Nonetheless, it did prevail. The deplorable conditions in Germany remained essentially unchanged until 1938. This was a decisive year for German Jewry. On April 26, the government declared that all Jews possessing property valued at more than 5,000 marks must declare their holdings by June 30th.[4] In May, a racial census was taken with the intent of clearly labeling the Jew. On June 9th, the Munich synagogue was destroyed by Nazi storm troopers,[5] and on June 15, there were wholesale arrests of Jews and other "anti-social" elements throughout Germany. It is estimated that at least two thousand were taken into custody with most being rushed off to concentration camps.[6] The press remained relatively silent.

---

[2] *The London Times*, September 16, 1935, p. 12.
[3] Editorial, *The New York Times*, September 17, 1935, p. 22.
[4] *The London Times*, April 27, 1938, p. 13.
[5] "Holocaust" *Encyclopedia Judaica*, 1st ed., vol. 3. (Jerusalem: Keter Publishing House, 1972), p. 828.
[6] *The London Times*, June 17, 1938, p. 15.

Evian, France, was the scene in mid-July of an International Refugee Conference. It was an excellent opportunity for the major powers to help provide a solution to the "Jewish" question. The *Diplomatische Politische Korrespondenz*, a semi-official organ of the German Foreign Office, very accurately commented upon both the attitude and results of this conference. It strongly proposed the following:

> Since in many foreign countries it was recently regarded as wholly incomprehensible why Germany did not wish to preserve in its population an element like the Jews because of their accomplishments, it appears astounding that these countries seem in no way particularly anxious to make use of this element themselves now that the opportunity offers. If these countries wish to take in some of these Jews, they can modify the immigration statutes they passed after the World War.[7]

As difficult as the first half of 1938 was for the Jew in Germany, the latter half proved to be far worse. August 10 saw the destruction of the Nuremberg Synagogue.[8] Due to the overwhelmlng influx of Jewish refugees, Switzerland closed its eastern and northern frontiers to all persons whose passports were not in order.[9] On August 17, the German government declared that any Jew whose personal name did not declare his non-Aryan blood, must add the name Israel or Sarah to that which he already possessed.[10] The *London Times* on October 6

---

[7] *The New York Times*, July 13, 1938, p. 12.
[8] *Encyclopedia Judaica*, p. 828.
[9] *The London Times*, August 19, 1938, p. 11.
[10] *The London Times*, August 20, 1939, p. 10.

(page 11) reported that in their desperation, thousands of Jews monthly were seeking passage to Australia with the intent of getting permission to stay. Simultaneously, the British Department of Interior warned shipping companies not to accept Jewish aliens as passengers without proof of permission to land, for they would not be admitted. On October 21, in a final move to cleanse the German courts, the government declared that after November 1, all licenses held by Jews to practice law would be revoked.[11] The front page of the *New York Times* on October 29 displayed the title, "Germany Deports Jews to Poland; Seizes Thousands." The article reported that at 5:00AM on October 28, the homes of Polish Jews living in Germany were raided and up to 18,000 Polish Jews were deported. The official reason given was that since the Polish government had decreed that on October 29 there might be some technical problem as to the validity of Polish passports, the German government did not want to lose their "right of expulsion" of Jews who might then be a burden for all time. It is indeed remarkable that during the above chain of events, not even one single editorial appeared in either the *New York* or *London Times.* Perhaps they felt that to continually rebuke the German government might seem redundant and make for "bad copy." This might very well be the case. However, it should be clear to every human being with even a latent moral sensitivity, that to sit back and merely chastise in the face of catastrophe is an outrage. Action!! Yes, action is what the moral soul cries out for. Action should have been the keynote of the editorial pages throughout the Nazi campaign. They should have been filled, not with rebuke for the Nazis, but rebuke for all the capitals of the world—to call for them to find a place in this universe for a vibrant yet defenseless people.

---

[11] *The London Times,* October 22, 1938, p. 11.

Paris, November 8, Herschel Grynsban, angered by the treatment of his fellow Jews, including the deportation of his parents to Poland, approached the German Embassy and executed the first official he saw. Reaction to the death of Herr Vom Rath, Third Secretary of the German Embassy in Paris, was predictable. The *London Times* on November 9 correctly prophesied that the shooting would certainly be a "signal for this fresh attack, which has been expected for some time."[12] On November 11, in a story entitled "Nazi Attacks on Jews" (page 14) the *London Times* reported: "The murder in Paris of Herr Vom Rath led in Germany today to scenes of systematic plunder and destruction which have seldom had their equal in a civilized country since the Middle Ages. In every part of the Reich, synagogues were set on fire or dynamited; Jewish shops smashed and ransacked and individual Jews arrested or hounded by bands of young Nazis through the streets."

In an editorial of that same day entitled "A Black Day for Germany," the *London Times* (page 15) expressed condemnation for the insane act of one "irresponsible and perhaps half-demented youth." However, it further commented about the futility of arousing world opinion that "the education of one people by the opinion of other peoples is an empty indulgence." But concerning the affront to Mr. Churchill in the German press, it strongly protested, "It is wholly intolerable. It demands official notice, and should receive it without delay." In other words, to protest the destruction of a whole people is an "empty indulgence," but when one individual suffers slander at the hands of a press that no one takes seriously anyway, this requires moral outrage.

The response of the *New York Times* to this *Kristalnacht*

---

[12] *The London Times*, November 9, 1938, p. 13.

was more sobering. In an editorial of November 11, entitled "Great Germany" (page 28), it observed:

> Thus does a great Government take revenge for the act of a maddened boy, a Government which exercises supreme and unquestioned power over 80,000,000 people, boasts of the order it maintains, and aspires to spread this order over all Central Europe. Recently this Government has extended its domain with the consent of the Western Powers, who acquiesced in its bloodless victories as the prelude to European appeasement. Instead, they were the prelude to the scenes witnessed yesterday, scenes which no man can look upon without shame for the degradation of his species.

Also in a *New York Times* November 12 editorial (page 14), entitled "Germany Forgets History," the following appeared:

> The present rulers of Germany can have learned nothing from the doom which fell upon their predecessors twenty years ago this week. The Imperial Government, between 1914 and 1918, repeatedly outraged neutral opinion by permitting its troops to run wild in Belgium; by the horror of its submarine campaign against passenger-carrying ships; and more than the acts themselves, by the gross stupidity with which it defended them. The German dictators of those days seemed to think that arrogance could beat down world opinion. It did not then. Can it now?

The *New York Times* was not without its share of prophecy. In its first response to the events of the *Kristalnacht*, it observed: "It is assumed that the Jews, who have now lost most of their possessions and livelihood, will either be thrown into the streets or put into ghettos and concentration camps, or impressed into labor brigades and put to work for the Third Reich as the children of Israel were once before for the Pharaohs.[13]

Stricter official measures were forthcoming. On November 12, the German Jewish community was told that they were to be further fined one billion marks in expiation for the murder of vom Rath. The Jewish shop owners had to repair the damages in their own stores, with the insurance claims proceeding to the government. Beginning with January 1, 1939, Jews were barred from operating retail mail order and handicraft establishments, and Jews could no longer be shop leaders directly in charge of personnel. Jews in leading positions in corporate businesses who were not shop leaders would be dismissed with six weeks' notice. Further drastic economic measures were promised. Possession of weapons by Jews would be punishable by imprisonment, Jews were also barred from theaters, movies, concerts, lectures halls and museums. They could no longer operate their newspapers or engage in any cultural or educational societies.[14] In Berlin, Jews were restricted from major sections of the city, forcing them into a ghetto type area. Jews were henceforth not permitted to own or operate automobiles. They were forced to wear yellow arm bands.[15] Many were soon to be found hiding in the woods outside the major cities, while the round-up of Jews for concentration camps proceeded.[16] As bad as it all seemed then, it was only a prelude to what was to follow.

In the aftermath of the *Kristalnach*, the *London Times*, in its long-awaited moment of sobriety, confronted the world with the following challenge:

---

[13] *The New York Times*, November 11, 1938, p. 1.
[14] *The New York Times*, November 13, 1938, p. 1.
[15] *The London Times*, December 4, 1938, p. 11.
[16] *The London Times*, November 14, 1938, p. 12.

It has too often been the practice of English-speaking democracies to denounce or to applaud the denunciation of the oppression of minorities and to warm themselves in the moral glow generated by the liberation of their emotions in the fond delusion that something has thus been done. In this, as in previous cases, deeds, not words, are required.

Fortunately, it can now be assumed that something is actually being done. (Note) the Prime Minister's statement that the question of finding a place in the Colonial Empire for Jewish refugees is being studied by the International Commission. These considerations, of course, give no excuse for unnecessary delay on the part of this country in taking its share in the solution of an urgent and pitiful problem. There is surely room for many of the refugees to settle in some part of the British Colonial Empire.[17]

It is not to be believed that the nations which feel this sympathy cannot find the means of assisting unwanted citizens to leave Germany and of providing the territory in which those Jews can found a liberated community and recover the right to live and prosper. There is no difficulty which a common will and common action cannot overcome.[18]

What happened to the Jewish people is well known. Six million died while the world remained relatively silent. Perhaps, if the press had spoken out with greater passion and conviction, millions of Jewish lives might have been saved.

—BR

---

[17]Editorial, *The London Times*, November 16, 1938, p. 15.
[18]Editorial, *The London Times*, November 17, 1938, p. 15.

16

The Secularization
and the DeJudaization
of the Holocaust

Fifty years after World War II a Holocaust Memorial Day is still not universally observed amongst the Jews of the world. When such a day is observed, the manner, essence and content of the commemoration ceremonies involved are subject to scrutiny, challenge and strong objections by both Jew and Gentiles alike, though for different reasons.

Many in the Orthodox Jewish community do not observe the Holocaust at all, some of them because they do not like to associate with the secular and non-orthodox elements within the Jewish community who are mainly involved with the Holocaust programs; others do not because the date of the Holocaust

Memorial Day has been set at the wrong time of the year and it conflicts with other major religious and historical dates on the Jewish calendar. Some still say that the entire manner in which the Holocaust is being observed is not in keeping with the very nature and tone of how Jews should observe such a unique event in Jewish history. In addition to these objections one must also add the fact that to date there is no evidence available that any rabbinical body ever went on record and made a formal proclamation instructing its adherents to observe a Holocaust Memorial Day by following a special program every year in the same month on the same day and in the same manner by all Jews. Even though the Rabbinical Assembly has inserted a special paragraph about the Holocaust in the *Shmoneh Esreh*, and Rev. Rosenfeld has composed and added some prayers about the *Shoah* to the *Kinnot* of Tishah B'Av (elegies about the Holocaust), the fact is that no rabbinical group has proclaimed the Holocaust as a special day on the Jewish calendar, let alone come out with a set ritual for the day.

The non-orthodox religious Jewish community that does observe the Holocaust does so either by having some kind of a short program consisting of selected reading of passages from the writing of Holocaust literature by Holocaust victims, or from the writings of post-Holocaust writers, a sermon or a speech, a few selections of passages from the prayer book and maybe the recitation of the kaddish. The secular Jews usually, if not all the time, involve Christian clergy in whatever Holocaust memorial program they have. (One must be puzzled and amazed by this development in Jewish life). This raises many problems and questions. What role can there be for non-Jewish people and especially clergy in a Jewish religious or even secular affair? If this practice is a subtle way of saying that the Holocaust is not a Jewish concern only, and that it is a matter concerning all humanity, then indeed what right do we have to claim that Jews should observe it or blame them for not observing it anymore than we do the Christians or the Muslims? But if Jews want to make the commemoration of the Holocaust tragedy into a significant Jewish religious experience or special secular event of an innately Jewish cultural nature, then why involve Christian clerics? The answer to this question can only be that these Jewish elements do not want to make these programs only Jewish in content, or do not think of the Holocaust as a particularly and uniquely Jewish phenomenon in history. Instead, they want to turn it into a kind of universal day of guilt expiation, moralizing and detachment from the Divine Presence in the affair of human and particularly Jewish history, and make the Holocaust an exclusive domain of the secular society. Furthermore, by bringing in Christian clergy, they think they will involve the world in better remembering the events of the Holocaust and thus prevent its reoccurrence.

Indeed that is the sad case. The Holocaust Memorial Day as we know it now was basically chosen, advocated, and implemented by the secular Zionist institutions of Israel, particularly through the creation of the Yad VaShem Museum in Israel and secular Jews in the United States and elsewhere. These elements of the Jewish people were and are removed from Jewish religious thinking and feeling. From the very beginning of choosing the date for commemorating the Holocaust to the most recent Holocaust museum that is being built somewhere in a Jewish community in a corner of the world, the Holocaust proponents in the Jewish community have and are always emphasizing the secular and excluding the religious experience of the Holocaust.

Soon after World War II when the Jewish leadership of Israel, the Jewish Agency, and all others who were involved in setting the tone of Jewish life at that time, chose the date for commemorating the Holocaust they did not have in mind what was in keeping with the sense of Jewish history, Jewish tradition and religious thinking, but rather what fit best into their political and ideological agenda. At that time their political agenda called for the secularization of the Jewish people, the advancement of the socialist Zionist goals and the institutionalization of their way of life. Thus the positive role of the Jewish religious leadership during the dark days of the Holocaust are ignored or at best barely mentioned, the heroism of many rabbis is overlooked, and instead they are singled out for criticism. They set the date for the Holocaust commemoration in order to commemorate the Warsaw Ghetto uprising that is especially connected with the Labor Zionist Circles who take credit for spearheading the Ghetto rebellion, and that marks an important moment in the history of the Holocaust particularly connected with Jewish physical resistance. In choosing this date, they on purpose or by implication ignore the very nature of the stoic, patient and dignified way in which ordinary Jews went to their death with faith in their hearts and a prayer for the future redemption of the Jews and all mankind, when the Messiah will come, on their lips. That is Jewish spiritual resistance par excellence. That indeed is true and historically unique Jewish heroism and not physical resistance, important though it may be at times.

The selection of the twenty-seventh of Nissan as the Holocaust memorial date ignored the Jewish calendar and Jewish tradition. The month of Nissan, because it is the month of the Festival of Passover, is set aside for rejoicing and not mourning. There are other days of the year when significant events took place during the Holocaust on which this memorial day could have been properly set. But the choice of this date was significant. It was meant to be a day for a secular gathering hailing the heroism of Jewish physical resistance exemplified by the Warsaw Ghetto Uprising, on the one hand, and the physical annihilation of the Jews in a world where the Divine presence is absent, on the other.

The emergence of Holocaust Memorial Programs in synagogues and temples is, relatively speaking, a recent development. Until recently such commemorative events were in the domain of public community groups such as Jewish Community Centers, Landsmaschaften of Survivors and other civic Jewish groups. Only as these groups began to decline and their influence in Jewish life started to recede did the synagogues and temples begin to play a more visible role in the area of Holocaust commemorative programs and fill the vacuum that was left in Jewish life. At the same time we also see the rise of Holocaust memorial centers appearing across the country and the world. These centers are by and large dominated by secular Jews, be they survivors or native American Jews. They are operated on the premise that the Holocaust is everybody's business, and that it is their mission in life to make sure that they must do everything in their power to prevent its reoccurrence. No one can really argue with this noble goal. But in order to achieve this goal they assume that they must involve the non-Jewish community. Ergo the thrust to incorporate the Christian clergy in the planning, implementation and execution of all Holocaust programs, and the operation of Holocaust memorial centers. Thus there are hardly Holocaust memorial museums or educational centers in existence that do not have some non-Jewish members and/or clergy on their boards of directors. The presence of non-Jews on the committees of these facilities has inevitably led to the question, "Why not include in the commemoration programs and activities references to the millions of non-Jews who were killed during the Holocaust era?"[1]

Indeed, partly in order to deal with this question, many of the programs and public pronouncements of the Holocaust Center dilute the specifically Jewish content in order to meet the requests of their non-Jewish members. Thus the time has come

---

[1] I am an eyewitness to such experiences.

when the message of the Holocaust seems to be no longer the story of the German program to annihilate the Jewish people from the face of the earth, but rather an act of Nazi brutality against humankind in general. The unique phenomenon of the German attempt to erase the Jews from the face of the earth, which is an unparalleled event in the annals of history, is lost in the shuffle to accommodate the feelings and wishes of non-Jewish well-meaning, and maybe not so well-meaning, people. The result is that Holocaust Memorial programs abound with secular commentaries and literary verbiage that is geared to have universal appeal. They involve Christian clergy to achieve maximum ecumenical effect, and presumably, to demonstrate Christian contrition for the events of the Holocaust on the one hand, and final acceptance of the Jew as an equal member of society on the other. However, as far as the ordinary people in the street are concerned, the participation and involvement of the Christian clergy in these functions only serves to lessen their consciousness of the Holocaust as a Jewish tragedy, and instead becomes a tool of heightening their awareness of the belief that the Holocaust was not a unique and solely Jewish tragedy, which proclaims the calamity of man's universal fall from grace and his self-demonization through his inhuman treatment of the Jew. Instead it becomes another event in history when men kill each other when they are at war, only this time they killed more.

It must also be noted that the involvement of non-Jews in the Holocaust committees, centers, and museums has not always been smooth sailing. Many times the incorporation of non-Jews in the Holocaust planning and leadership positions, though intended to bring about greater understanding between Jews and Christians, leads to tension and friction between the participants. These arguments are invariably over the question of whether or not to include the non-Jewish victims of German criminal atrocity and mass murder in the same category as the

Jewish people and apply the term *Holocaust* to all of them equally, or to use it as a term which describes the unique German attempt to destroy only the Jews. These arguments often culminate in, at best, new animosity, and, at worst, charges of Jewish exclusivity and superiority and counter charges of anti-semitism between the participants. Thus, this seemingly well-intentioned attempt to bring Jews and Gentiles together becomes the cause of tearing them apart.

It is unfortunate that the way Holocaust memorial committees and programs are now constituted, they run against the very essence of good Jewish taste and religious sensitivity. Instead of developing during the last fifty years since World War II a meaningful Holocaust rite, those in the Jewish community who are involved with the Holocaust used it, and continue to use it, to advance their own ideological and political agendas, to strip it of any religious meaning, and to promote some undefined notions of a future edifice of a secular humanitarian good and brotherhood of man built upon the ashes of the Holocaust victims. They deal with it in a superficial and temporary fashion. They do not take into consideration the true Jewish feelings, traditional life style and faith of the victims. They portray them as though they were all secular and politically correct people judged by contemporary politically correct standards of conduct. They forget or ignore the fact that the Jews of the Holocaust era were very much steeped in Jewish tradition and values, regardless of whether or not they still practiced all the Jewish ritual. Of these Jewish values and rituals, the most universally believed in, and observed, were those associated with death, burial rites and their related religious services. This is never, or at the very best, barely reflected in the programs and activities of the Holocaust committees and museums. Instead they work on programs that meet their momentary fancy or mood, without giving it any philosophical or ethical depth of lasting value. Nothing is done to last beyond the given moment. Though the people who work on Holocaust programs are well-meaning, committed, hard working and wonderful people, their well-intentioned programs will not endure, because they are not grounded in the life, faith and traditional beliefs of the average Jewish person.

—CR

17

Jewish Memorial Days
and the Holocaust

The Jewish calendar is full of memorial days. These memorial days commemorate the disasters that befell the Jewish people in the course of their long history. The question, therefore, arises, "Why have the Jews not established a memorial day that is universally observed by all the Jews throughout the world in memory and honor of the six million Jews who were killed by the Germans and their collaborators during World War II?"

An examination of the nature and historical context of the various memorial days that Jews are observing may provide us with an explanation of the intrinsic nature of what constitutes a Jewish Memorial Day, and give us the reasons why there is no memorial day for our six million martyrs that is universally observed by all the Jews.

Jewish memorial days can be divided into three distinct groups. These are: memorial days based on catastrophic events that befell the Jewish people in biblical times; memorial days that commemorate catastrophes that befell entire Jewish communities encompassing a whole country or city in exile; and memorial days that individual people or families are observing in memory of specific tragedies that happened to them or their ancestors.

The biblical memorial days can be divided into two parts, one, those that are explicitly mentioned in the Torah, and those that were instituted by the rabbis before the destruction of the Second Temple. The memorial days that are mentioned in the Torah are Pesach, Succoth (including Sh'minni Atzereth), and Shavu'oth. (We mention Shavu'oth because in the strict sense of the word it too is a commemorative festival, as it commemorates the Giving of the Torah on Mount Sinai. It is not germane to our discussion unless one cynically argues that indeed that was the greatest tragedy that befell the Jewish people, because from that moment on, the Jews were singled out to be responsible to carry the burden of the Divine commandments and always be a light unto the nations.) The memorial days that were instituted by the rabbis are Purim, Chanukah and Chamishah Assar B'shvat. (Chamishah Assar B'shvat is a memorial day only because it is the New Year of the Trees, and in the sense that it celebrates God's control over nature, and shows how the entire universe is interrelated. It is strictly speaking not germane to our discussion.)

All of these memorial days have the following elements in common: They celebrate the Divine redemption and salvation of the Jew from suffering, oppression and immminent annihilation at the hands of their enemies. In the case of the memorial days mentioned in the Torah, the enemy was Pharaoh and the Egyptian nation on Pesach, and the nations of the Sinai Peninsula, especially Amalek on Succoth. In the case of Purim, the enemy was Haman and his cohorts. In the case of Chanukkah the enemy was Alexander Epiphaness and the Hellenists. Thus we see that even in the cases underlying the biblical and rabbinical memorial days there is a history of suffering. The Torah and the rabbis, however, did not choose to dwell on the negative experiences and the suffering of the Jews. Instead they chose to emphasize the good. That is, the Torah and the rabbis took those dangerous moments in the history of the Jewish people, and turned them from days of sadness and gloom into days of gladness and joy. Thereby they also taught us how full of mercy God is for having saved our ancestor from certain destruction, and giving them life. They also taught us how much we are dependent on the grace of God for our daily existence. These commemorative days of the Torah emphasize not the fact that we suffered, but the fact that we survived. They teach us the virtue of Hakkarat Tov—the need to acknowledge the good that is done to us. In that case we are taught that we should not take for granted the good that we experience. Instead we should look upon it as a gift of God.

There are additional rabbinical memorial days that are classified as fast days. These are Tzom G'dali'yahu, Assarah B'Tevet, Ta'anith Esther, Shiva Assar B'Tamuz and Tishah B'Av. (Even though Tishah B'Av is in a category of its own, it falls in the same classification. It only differs in the intensity and strictness of its observance.) All of these memorial days commemorate tragic events in the history of the Jewish people. They are observed more or less in the same manner by the recitation of special penitential prayers, reading from the Torah a special selection that deals with God's admonition to the Jews to obey His laws and not to stray from them, and an insertion of a special petitional prayer into the Amidah, asking God to show us His mercy on this, the day of fasting. On Tishah B'Av, the Scroll of Lamentations is also read during the evening services.

Underlying these commemorative days of fasting and their services are the following elements, from which we may learn many things about the classical Jewish *weltanschaung* and its perspective on suffering and mourning. The first is mourning. The Jews mourn the pain and tragedy that they suffered at the hands of their oppressors. Another is identification. The Jews identify with their ancestors and feel the pain and anguish of their forebears as though they themselves experienced those dreadful and awesome events. The third is Divine retribution. The Jews regard these calamities that came upon them as Divine retribution for the sins of the Jewish people. The fourth is guilt. The Jews look upon themselves as being responsible for and having brought upon themselves these tragedies because they have not followed in God's ways. The Jews see themselves as being guilty in their own eyes for having violated God's commandments. The fifth is that the prayers and fasting on these memorial days are in and of themselves admissions of guilt. The sixth is restitution. By observing these Memorial Fast Days, the Jews believe that they can make up for the sins of their people. The seventh element is that God is forgiving. The Jews believe that if they recognize the errors of their ways and acknowledge their sins, God will forgive them. The eighth is reconciliation. God and the Jews will be reconciled because of the fact that the Jews atone for their sins. Consequently, there will be a reconciliation between God and the Jews. The Jews will return to God and God will return to the Jews. The ninth consideration is restoration. The Jews will be restored to their ancient glory. The tenth deals with faith and hope. Underlying the observance of these Fast Days is an abiding faith in God, in the fact that there is a reason for all that takes place in the history of the Jewish people and a conviction that even though the Jews may be in exile, God is always nigh to them and waiting for their return to Him. Concomitant with this comes an unwavering hope that sooner or later God will redeem his people and restore them to their rightful place.

Two additional characteristics of all the biblical and rabbinical memorial days are: (1) at the point in time when the tragic events that are being commemorated took place, they did so in the presence of all the Jewish people at one and the same time. In other words, all the Jews at that time were equally involved and affected by what took place. There was no one Jew or Jewish community that could claim that it was outside the scope of the tragedy that was taking place; (2) All those events took place either when the Jews were in one place, that is, Egypt, or the wilderness of Sinai, or in their own land, The Land of Israel.

The second distinct group of Jewish memorial days deals with post-biblical tragedies that befell entire Jewish communities. These tragedies, whether they encompassed only one city or an entire country, fall into two groups, which are those that are commemorated only by the residents of those localities where the tragedies occurred, and those that are commemorated as part of the general observance of other memorial days. The post-biblical history of the Jewish people is replete with tragedy after tragedy, yet we find relatively few memorial days that are set aside to commemorate the victims of those tragedies. Several noteworthy exceptions, nevertheless, do exist.

In the category of local or regional memorial days, one must take into account the fast day of the twentieth day of Sivan.[1] That day is a day of fasting and supplication for the Jewish people who were killed during the Ukrainian uprising, led by Bogdan Chmelnitzky against the Polish rule during the years 1648 to 1649. During that short period of time over three hundred thousand Jews were killed.

Thousands more were maimed, taken into slavery and the

---

[1] Avraham Segol, *Magen Avraham, Maginei Eretz, Shulchan Aruch, Orach Chaim,* pt. 3 (Warsaw: The Brothers and Partners, 1877), sect. 580, sub-section 3.

women sold as wives to those who would have them. The glorious period of Jewish life in those Slavic countries that saw the reign of a Jewish king in Poland, and the period of Jewish autonomy known as the time of the Va'ad Arba'ah Artzot, when the Jews of the Baltic, Ukrainian, Polish and Galician lands ruled their own lives, came to a tragic end.[2] In memory of, and in mourning for this savage destruction of the Jewish communities the surviving rabbinical leadership designated the twentieth day of Sivan as a day of mourning and fasting throughout the lands where this terrible devastation of the Jewish people took place. They chose that date because it never falls on a Sabbath and therefore the fast will never be changed to another day, such as Thursday. They chose that time of the year because that time of the year seems to be a time when bad things happen to the Jews.[3] The twentieth day of Sivan was observed as a fast day throughout the Polish communities until they themselves were destroyed by the Germans and their collaborators during World War II.

The purpose of the fast of the twentieth day of Sivan was to mourn and to lament for the loss of the Jews during those terrible slaughters of the years 1648 to 1649 and to atone for the sins of our people that led to that horrible tragedy.[4]

We learn from this fast day the following salient points: The Jewish people did institute public memorial days to commemorate the destruction of Jewish communities; the memorial day is limited in observance to the people of the same country (the descendants of the martyrs), and to countries where the tragedy took place; and in order to be able to establish such a memorial day, there are several conditions that are necessary. There should

---

[2]S. M. Dubov, *History of the Jews in Russia and Poland*, vol 1., I. Friedlander, trans. (Philadelphia: The Jewish Publication Society, 1916), pp. 144–158.
[3]*Magen Avraham*, op. cit.
[4]Ibid.

be an authoritative rabbinical body or rabbi whose authority is accepted by the people, and there has to be a surviving remnant willing to be guided and indeed looking toward the rabbis to lead and guide them. In spite of the devastation that took place in the years 1648–49, there still remained some Jewish community life and a remnant of Jews who were able and willing to accept rabbinical leadership and decisions. There also remained some great rabbis who were both able and willing to render decisions in behalf of their Jewish communities.[5]

Unfortunately, not all Jewish communities were blessed enough to leave any survivors. That brings us to the second category of post-biblical memorial days.

From the days of antiquity through the tenth century, there were thriving Jewish communities in the Middle East. Those were the communities of what is today modern Iran, Iraq and Egypt. Those were the communities where rabbinical Judaism thrived, where the Talmud came into being, and where the foundation was laid for Jewish life in the exile. All of these communities came to a tragic end, whether because of sudden disasters that came upon them or gradual destruction brought upon them by the forces of death, forced conversion and expulsion. The end result was that those communities disappeared. No memorial days are known to be observed or to have been established in their memory in the lives of European Jewry.

During the crusades great devastation took place in the Jewish communities of Europe. The crusaders pillaged and ravaged, and left in their wake death and ashes. The Rheinland Jewish communities were wiped out. The Jews of England were exploited, tortured and expelled. The most notable event in the destruction of Anglo Jewry is the self-immolation of the Jews of York in 1189 in an act of selfless martyrdom and defiance. Years

---

[5]Ibid.

later we have the Spanish Inquisition and the expulsion of the
Jews from Spain in 1492. These were cataclysmic times in the
history of the Jewish people. We have no record of any memorial
day that was set aside to commemorate these events.[6]

In the *kinnot* (dirges) for Tishah B'Av there are several
kinnot inserted in memory of the Jews who were killed and the
Jewish communities of the Rheinlands that were destroyed
during the crusades, and a *kinnah* for the martyrs of York.[7]
Other than that, there are no memorial days observed by the
Jews of the Middle East, England, the Rheinland and Spain to
commemorate the destruction of their ancient and not so ancient
Jewish communities and the murder of their ancestors.

The reason for that is obvious. There were no Jews left in
those countries to establish and to observe memorial days. Based
on what we have said about the fast day of the twentieth day of
Sivan, it is now clear that memorial days for our martyrs in the
post-biblical period of our history were established only by the
survivors of the devastated communities. Where there were no
survivors, there were no memorial days.

Jews who were fortunate enough to live in countries where
there were no destructions either did not identify strongly
enough with their brethren of the destroyed communities, or did
not feel that it was incumbent upon them to fast and mourn the
destruction of fellow Jews from different countries. Perhaps, it

---

[6]Ibid. Here it is mentioned that the twentieth day of Sivan was also
set aside to commemorate the Jews who were killed during the
crusades.

[7]Elegy on the Martyrs of York by Joseph Chartres. *Kinnot for the
Ninth of Av, The Tisha B'Av Compendium*, trans. and annotated by
Rabbi Abraham Rosenfeld (New York: The Judaica Press, 1986), p.
168. This book also contains the *Kinnot for the Martyrs of the
Crusades*. See p. 132 to 134. It also said that the expulsion of the
Jews from Spain took place on Tishah B'Av.

may also be said that memorial days fall in the category of days of personal mourning, such as Yahrzeits, that are observed and kept only by relatives. Indeed, one may not impose one's own mourning on others, namely the public. Jews from countries where there was no destruction may have felt that since they were not related, as a group, to the Jews who were destroyed in a different country, that therefore they did not have a duty to institute and impose a memorial day upon their own communities. Such a day would have been essentially a time of mourning for strangers from a foreign land. Only when there were no survivors left, did other communities include some reference to those who were destroyed into the already established order of prayers for existing fast days.[8] One may, therefore, wonder whether or not the special *kinnot* for the communities of the Rheinland and that of York would have been inserted into the prayers of Tishah B'Av if there would have been any survivors, who then would have had to declare their own day of fasting for the dead Jews of their country.

The third category of memorial days is the one that was established by individuals, families or small groups to commemorate events that occurred in their lives. Such days consist of fasting and giving thanks to God for His mercy and saving grace for having redeemed the survivors in question from the trouble that they faced. A noted case in point of such a memorial day is recorded by Rabbi Avraham Danziger in his monumental work, the *Chay'ye Adam*, Principle 150, in which he states that on the sixteenth day of Kislev, 5564, a great explosion took place in the courtyard in which he and his family lived. Thirty-one people were killed and there was not a member of his family that was not wounded. In commemoration of this event, he and his family

---

[8]As in the case of the inclusion of *kinnot* about York into those of Tishah B'Av.

observe the sixteenth day of Kislev as a fast day. "Those who can should fast on that day."[9] We learn from the practice of this saintly rabbi that, indeed, it is proper to commemorate one's own experiences, and to set aside days for fasting and atonement in conjunction with the trouble that one has lived through.

We may now summarize the basic requirements for the institution of a public memorial day as well as what constitutes a memorial day.

In biblical times and soon thereafter in the rabbinical period of Jewish history, a memorial day was instituted in order to celebrate the redemption of the Jewish people from any impending disaster. The memorial day commemorated the salvation of the Jews and the downfall of their enemies. In rabbinical times, fast days were established in order to mourn the destruction of Jewish communities and atone for the sins of the Jews. The fast days are then an affirmation of the faith of the Jews in God's providence and in the Jew's responsibility for the trouble that came upon him.

In later post-rabbinical times, memorial days were established by the survivors of ravished communities to mourn the death of their kinsmen and members of their countries who were killed.[10]

Jews in exile did not institute public memorial days for Jews

---

[9]Avraham Danziger, *Sefer Cha'ye Adam*, Klal 150, *The Laws of the Megillah*, section 41. Jerusalem: 1990, p. 693–694. Rabbi Danziger also states that he chose that date as a proper day for fasting because it is a day on which some Jews are already fasting anyway.
[10]Dates known to be those on which bad things happened to the Jews in the past were usually chosen as fast days to commemorate recent tragedies. This practice is based on the principle that we should not increase the number of bad days in our calendar. See *Magen Avraham*, op. cit.

of different countries.[11] However, Jews have often established commemorative fast days to mark events that happened to them or their families.

How does all of this apply to the commemoration of the Jews who were killed by the Germans and their collaborators during World War II?

What were the conditions of the destruction of European Jewry?

All the Jewish communities of Europe were destroyed! There were no organized Jewish communities left in Europe after the war (except in England!) There were no rabbinical authorities left in Europe after the war! There were no organized Jewish groups who were willing or able to accept any rabbinical decree to observe any memorial day or fast day for the killed Jews of Europe! After World War II European Jewry was dead! Like the Jewish communities of long ago in Iran, Iraq, Egypt, the Rheinlands, York, Spain, they too had no one left to commemorate them and to mourn them. Those Jews who survived were like the proverbial piece of wood that was plucked out of the fire like a burned piece of coal. As individuals and as small groups they did what they could to say kaddish or observe *yizkor* for their dead parents and other kin. Many of the survivors were bitter, angry at man and at God. Many are still angry today, fifty years later. Jewish life, such as it was after the war, was controlled by the Zionist movement that was itself anti religious and hostile to Judaism and Jewish religious practices. They certainly were

---

[11]Individuals, however, did fast because of tragedies that befell Jewish communities. See the *Shulchan Aruch, Orach Chaim* 3, sect. 580, sub-section 3, and the Be'er Haytiv on that part. It is possible that the fast days referred to in the *Orach Chaim* were declared to be proper days on which one should fast because on those days the Torah and the Temple were burned, which is of a personal concern to every Jew.

not going to institute a fast day or a religious memorial day. The Jews who survived the war were in no mood to turn to fasting and accepting any responsibility for the tragedy that overtook the Jewish people. They were in a state of depression, rejection, spiritual rebellion, and in no way prepared or amenable to talk about sin and Divine retribution. They could not fathom how God stood by and allowed the gruesome and brutal destruction of European Jewry, among them saints and scholars, infants and old, men and women alike! After surviving the hell and damnation of World War II the Jews of Europe did not exist as a spiritual entity anymore! How could they be expected to establish fast days and memorial days! Their very existence was a living memorial!

But what about the Jews of the rest of the world? What about the Jews of Israel, Latin America, Australia, Canada, South Africa and the United States of America? What have they done to commemorate the destruction of a third—six million—of the Jewish people?

Given what we have said before, it would seem that the Jews of the rest of the world do not have any obligation to establish a fast day or a memorial day for the Jews who were killed in Europe. After all, that took place outside their countries. The question, though, that must be asked is, "Were the Jews from the rest of the world excluded from the attempt to exterminate the Jews? Did the Germans and their cohorts intend to kill only the European Jews and not any other Jews who lived outside of Europe?" If this were so, Jews from outside of Europe might argue that since only the Jews of Europe were killed, then they have no obligation to decree a fast day and a memorial day for those who were killed in Europe. The facts, however, are pointing in another direction altogether. The Germans and their collaborators planned and intended to kill all the Jews of the entire world. It was an accident of history that the Jews of Europe were killed and not the other Jews. They were killed because they were there. Had the other Jews been there, they would have been killed first. Had Germany won the war, then all the Jews of all the other countries would have been killed also. Therefore, all the Jews are in this sense survivors of the war! As survivors it is incumbent upon them to establish a fast day and memorial day for the Jews who perished in the war no less than it was incumbent upon the Jews who survived the massacres of 1648 to 1649 to establish a fast day on the twentieth day of Sivan.

The questions are, "Are they capable of doing it or not? Do they have the religious conviction that would compel them to turn to God? Do they have the rabbinical leadership that would direct them and guide them to do it?"

After the war the Jews of the world lacked the most important components that are required for the institution of new fast days and memorial days. They did not have the authoritative and well-accepted rabbinical leaders who were either able to make decrees or who were accepted by the religious Jewish community so that their decrees would have been accepted. There was no one who could or would take it upon himself to call upon the Jews to commemorate the murdered Jews. When the great rabbis of Europe were killed, world Jewry was left without any rabbinical leadership of world stature. The Jews of the world after the war were either anti-religious or religiously impotent to do anything. The anti religious Jews were either assimilated or mainly involved with the building of the Jewish state. Memorial days and fast days were not on their agenda. The religious Jews were divided into many groups, not one of which took it upon itself to call upon its followers to observe a fast day or to establish a memorial day, either to mourn those who died or to give thanks for those who survived. It must also be said that at the very least it is highly questionable how much, if at all, the Jews outside of Europe have identified themselves with the catastrophe that befell the Jews of

Europe, and how much they ever accepted the truth that "there but for the grace of God go I" applied to them as individuals and as a group. Perhaps if they would have done so, they might have reacted differently to the tragedy and done something about it. Perhaps their inaction has also something to do with the fact that they did so little during the war to help their lost and forlorn brethren of Europe. Of course we speak mainly about the Jews of the United States, because of all the Jewish communities in the world they were, as they continue to be, the mightiest. Now if they did not do anything, what then could have been expected of the other Jewish communities of the world? If the Jews of America did not empathize with the slaughter that was taking place in Europe why should the Jews of more distant lands have done so?

Maybe instead of asking why has world Jewry, and especially American Jewry, not established any fast day or memorial day in memory of the Jews who were exterminated by the Germans during World War II, we should ask why world Jewry, and especially American Jewry, have not identified more intimately with the lot of the Jews of Europe? Had they done so we would not have had to worry about any other question.

—*CR*

18

The Lost Jews of the *Shoah*

During the recent elections in Poland, some political figures who seemingly were not Jewish, were accused by their opponents of being Jewish, as though that were a crime in and of itself. This example of recrudescent anti-semitism was met by an outcry of "Foul!", and the astonished chagrin of Jews and some well-meaning people of the West. The Jews and other people were surprised, hurt, pained and taken aback. They and many other people were shocked that fifty years after World War II, and after all that Poland itself suffered at the hands of the Germans and the communist regime, that there still remained in Poland so much hostility to the Jews, to the point that anti-semitism became a politically convenient tool. They, naturally, reacted strongly with condemnations and calls for proper action on the part of the Polish government and church authorities to combat and remove anti-semitism from Poland.

Unfortunately there is more than one side to this story. It is correct that there is a recrudescent anti-semitism in Poland. For that matter it is not even recrudescent because it was always there, before, during, and now after the German occupation and the communist rule. It never disappeared. It is also true that this is no excuse that it should continue to be an integral or any other part of the Polish social order. It is also true that civilized society should not stand by and allow anti-semitism to be used as a political tool to disqualify people from standing for election because they are Jewish. However, it was also said that the people who were accused of being Jewish were not. It was assumed that the anti-Semites thought that by merely accusing someone of being a Jew that that person would lose the election. Now this is the difficult part: There may have been some truth to this story, because the people who were accused of being Jewish, though they themselves never considered themselves as Jews, may in fact have been Jewish or descended from Jews without even being aware of it themselves. However, their neighbors, relatives and friends from the elder generation may have been aware of this. In other words, the Poles know who comes from a Jewish background or is a Jew even if the Jewish person himself or herself no longer knows, either because he or she has forgotten, or is subconsciously suppressing it. The truth is that there may be some truth to the accusation that these politicians either are Jewish or descend from Jews, even if they themselves no longer know it. That is the other sad and tragic part of the *Shoah.*

I have personally come across people and heard accounts of Jews who were lost in the process of trying to save their lives. These Jews are now living as Poles or other nationals wherever they are.

From 1945 to 1946, when I lived in a children's kibbutz in the Displaced Persons camp in Landsberg, Germany, there was among us a young boy who must have been no more than thirteen years old. He was called Marek. He was from Poland. He was always in trouble, fighting, arguing and cursing the Jews with the finest repertoire of the worst kind of anti-Semite. I remember how our counsellors asked us to be nice to him and to make him welcome because he was hidden by a Polish family during the war. Now he was bought (ransomed) by the Jewish community. While living with the Poles, he had been indoctrinated with a hatred of the Jews and anything Jewish. In time, the counsellors said to us, he will forget this hatred of the Jews and he will become one of us. In the meantime, Marek was going around cursing the Jews, holding on to his ring that had the engraving of an big eagle, the national Polish symbol, and asking to be returned to his Polish home and parents. Marek went to what was then Palestine. But how many Mareks were not ransomed by the Jewish community and remained with their new Polish, Ukrainian, Belorussian, and other parents who inculcated them with a hatred of the Jewish people? How many of these children are today parents and grandparents whose children are members of their communities, and are leaders of their countries without even remembering that they were born Jews or knowing that their father or mother is or was a Jew? How many of them are being accused of being Jewish without knowing why? How many of them are reminded by their neighbors that they are Jews? How many of them are anti-Semites themselves?

Years later when I lived in Winnipeg, Manitoba, Canada from 1948 to 1952, I used to be a very regular visitor in the home of my revered mentor and teacher, Rabbi Abraham Kravetz, of blessed memory. I remember well how upset he would become when he would read in the Jewish press how some Jewish Orthodox organizations would claim how much they did and are doing to help to save the survivors of the *Shoah*.

He was particularly upset with and angry at the previous Lubavitcher Grand Rabbi, because when Rabbi Kravetz was the Chief Rabbi of Lodz, Poland, he tried to ransom Jewish children from the Polish families that managed to save them during the war. There were many such children. These Jewish children were entrusted into the care of the Polish families for safety and protection from the Germans. The parents of these children were killed. They had no one left. Now many Polish families were willing to return these children for money to the Jews. There was no one to claim them except the Jewish community. But the Jewish community was decimated. Only the various Jewish Aid agencies, the Zionist movements and the religious organizations were in some position to help. Rabbi Kravetz turned to the Grand Rabbi of Lubavitch for help. The Grand Rabbi always promised to send him the money for the ransom of these children, but it never came. Time after time arrangements were made for one child after another child to be redeemed and the money never came. In America these organizations were proclaiming how much they were doing for the Jews who survived the war, and in Poland these children remained with their Polish families.

Who can count the number of Jewish children who were lost among the nations of Europe as a result of their parents' desperate attempts to save them from the German butchers?

Many years later (in the mid-1980s) when I served as a rabbi in Orlando, Florida, I was called upon to attend to the needs of a family whose relative died while in Orlando. This person and family were not known to me personally, so I had to make some inquiries about them. This is what I found out about them. The deceased and his wife were Polish Jews. They were survivors of the war. They had a daughter who was married. All the years after the war, they had nothing to do with any Jewish community or the Jewish people as a whole. When I asked, "Is their daughter married to a Jew?", I was told that she doesn't even know that she herself is Jewish. In response to my next question "Why not?" I was told that her parents were so shaken by the German attempt to kill all the Jews that they were living in constant fear that it might happen again. To save themselves and especially their daughter from future and present anti-Semites, they decided not to tell her that they were Jews.

This is not an isolated story. Other Jews felt the same way after the war. I remember my own cousin Steven Dell (Shayeh Delatitzki) telling me that when he was liberated from the Dachau Concentration Camp at the age of seventeen, he felt like running away as far as possible from any Jew, living among the Gentiles and never acknowledging that he was a Jew. He did not run far. But many did.

We shall never know how many endless numbers of Jews did not tell their children that they are Jewish. We shall never know how many Jews ran away from us never to return. Are they not also the victims of the *Shoah* whom the Germans took away from us and killed? Surely this is so if only in the spiritual sense!!

As a rabbi in England I heard about the *kindertransport*, which was the rescue effort to bring Jewish children from Germany to England just before the borders between England and Germany were closed. Many of these children were brought to England and placed in Gentile homes, never again to return to the Jewish people. Today there are many people who are part and parcel of the English population and are members of the Anglican Church. Some of them may still have faint memories of their Jewish childhood, Jewish parents, and Jewish relatives. Their children, specially if the mother is Jewish, are also Jewish. They hardly have an inkling that their father or mother is Jewish. Some day they may be reminded by some anti-Semite that they are Jewish and they will wonder why. We have a very good idea of how many Jews were killed. We will never know how many Jews were taken from us never to return, and how many left us because of fear, and still how many more just never came back. These are the Jews who perished in the other *Shoah*.

The Midrash tells us that when Aaron's two elder sons died by fire, their bodies were untouched and left intact. Only their souls were destroyed. To this day Jews read on Yom Kippur the portion of the Torah that tells us about this event in order to remind us of that great tragedy.

The Jewish men, women and children who never came back to us are like the sons of Aaron. Though their bodies remained untouched, their souls were consumed forever. As we do for Aaron's sons, we shall always remember and mourn them.

—CR

19

By Whose Leave?

The builders of Holocaust museums and centers and their followers promulgate the theory that the victims of the Holocaust will not have died in vain, if only mankind will learn from their death how wicked and evil their destruction was, and if, as a result of this, man will abolish all racial, religious and national bigotry, hatred, prejudice, racism, and strife from the midst of all social, national and international life. If this will be accomplished, then one might conclude that the Holocaust was not in vain and the victims did not die an empty death.

To better understand and analyze this theory, it is necessary to know the philosophy of life upon which it is based.

The basic principles that underpin this hypothesis are: If mankind will know what kind of evil it perpetrated upon the Jews and how wicked and inhuman it is for humankind to act in that manner, it will change its ways for the better; we should tell the world how badly it treated the Jews during the Holocaust and it will become a better world; if, as a result of what happened during the Holocaust, the world will become a better place to live in for all people, then the victims of the Holocaust will not have died in vain; and it is all right to die in order to serve some greater cause than one's own life. The Holocaust fulfills this requirement. Or does it?

Jewish history is full of martyrs and martyrdom. There are three particular event that took place in the course of our long suffering and martyred existence from which we might learn how to understand and relate to the mind-boggling and heartbreaking nightmare of the Holocaust.

The Talmud tells us that in the days of the Hadrianic oppressions, there were two brothers, Julian and Julianus. Although they had a checkered reputation during their lifetime because they were identified as what today might be called terrorists or freedom fighters, depending on what one's perspective of life might be, attained the virtue of being totally righteous people, in whose presence in Heaven nobody could stand.

What was the merit of these two brothers?

According to the Talmud[1] the story is that in the town of Lud, a Roman princess was found dead. In order to apprehend the perpetrators of the crime, the Romans proclaimed that unless those who committed the crime were handed over to them, they would kill all the Jews of Lud. In order to save the entire Jewish population of the town, Julian and Julianus, even though they

---

[1] *Baba Batra* 10a and *Pesachim* 50a, (Vilna: The Widow and Brothers Romm, 1920).

were innocent, surrendered themselves to the Roman authorities and claimed to have killed the princess. They were, of course, executed.

There are three basic elements to the virtuous, noble and self-sacrificing act of those two brothers. First, no one was forcing them to surrender and die. They acted voluntarily, that is to say, they committed their act of heroism as a conscious choice which they made. They had a choice. They could have kept quiet and lived. They chose to die in order to save the people of Lud. Second, their self-sacrifice saved the people of the city of Lud. There was an immediate and tangible result to their death. Third, the decision to live or die was their own.

In the liturgy of Yom Kippur and Tishah B'Av we read about the *Assarah Harugay Malchut* (The Ten Martyrs of Faith)[2] including the great Rabbi Akiva. This event also took place during the great Hadrianic oppression of the Jewish people, when the Romans prohibited the study and practice of Judaism and put to gruesome death whomever they caught disobeying their edict. The great sages continued to teach the Torah in spite of the Roman prohibitions and in full knowledge that if they were caught, they would face certain death. They were caught and killed. Now they are rightfully revered as martyrs of the Jewish faith.

Like the two brothers, they too made a conscious choice. They knew what awaited them. They had to choose. They could stop the teaching of the Torah and live, or they could continue to teach the Torah and die. They chose to teach and to die.

---

[2] See Talmud *Avodah Zara* 17b–18a, *Berachot* 61b, *Pesachim* 50a, *Sanhedrin* 13b–14a (Vilna: The Widow and Brothers Romm, 1920) and Lamentations *Rabbah* 2:4. Midrash Rabbah Hamvuar, Aycha Rabbati, (Jerusalem: Machon HaMidrash Hamvuar, 1990). For the elegy see *Tisha B'av Compendium*, translated and annotated by Rabbi Abraham Rosenfeld (New York: The Judaica Press, 1986), p. 125–126.

In later years, specifically during the Middle Ages, thousands of Jews died as martyrs. These Jews also had a choice. They could have become apostates and converted to Islam or Christianity, and lived. Instead they chose to die as Jews. They too are called martyrs of the faith whose death and self-sacrifice, like that of the Ten Martyrs of the Faith, is a shining example for all ages of Jewish martyrdom and commitment to the faith of our fathers. The Jewish martyrs of the Middle Ages who died rather than convert also had a choice. They made a conscious decision to die as Jews rather than to live as apostates.

The common denominator of all Jewish martyrs through the ages consisted of (1) confronting a choice between life and death, (2) making a conscious choice to die rather than let other people die, or give up one's commitment to studying the Torah and thus one's faith in God, and, (3) dying as Jews rather than living as apostates. In addition to these factors, Jewish martyrdom was always public, that is, other people knew about it and saw it take place. Most of all, it was an exemplary act that was capable of being imitated. In short, it was meant to be a deed that others, given the same circumstances, could imitate and thus act in a similar heroic fashion. In other words, all martyrdom must be capable of being emulated.[3]

These criteria of Jewish martyrdom cannot be applied to the victims of the Holocaust. The Holocaust victims were not given any choice. They were not told to accept apostasy or die; they

---

[3]Menachem Begin points out in his autobiographical book, *White Knights,* how martyrdom had no meaning to him when he was being interrogated by the Russian Secret Police in Vilna because he was in total isolation. He had no contact with and no knowledge of the outside world, nor the outside world of him. Therefore any act of heroic martyrdom in the face of the Russian torturers had no purpose, because it would never be known to the world, and in order for one to act as a martyr, one's act must be public.

were not told to stop studying the Torah or die; and they certainly did not and could not save anyone from death by dying themselves. Most certainly what happened in the Holocaust is not to serve as an example for others to imitate even if it was performed in public, and not only some people, but also whole nations knew about it. To imitate the Holocaust is, by virtue of what it was, beyond imagination and human nature. For, taken to its logical conclusion, if the Holocaust would not have been stopped by the Allied victory, there would not have remained any Jews to allow themselves to be killed in the future in order to imitate the virtuous acts of self-sacrifice of the Holocaust victims.

How then do we define the Holocaust and how do we relate to the victims? What place does it occupy in Jewish history and do we have any precedents that might enable us to better understand and cope with the trauma of the Holocaust?

Jewish history, unfortunately, is full of martyrdom, death, ruination, self sacrifice, and, by the grace of God, also resurrection and survival. Two momentous events from our past come to mind. These events might shed some light on, and give us some direction on how to face the Holocaust, which is the darkest chapter of our long, tortured, though often glorious, journey in time.

The first one is that of the *Akaydah*, the attempted sacrifice of Isaac. This is one of the most moving and awe inspiring stories of the Torah. The Book of Genesis[4] tells us that in order to test Abraham's faith, God tells him to sacrifice his only beloved son Isaac at Mount Moriah. Abraham, without the slightest hesitation, takes his son and together they go for a three day's journey to Mount Moriah. Finally upon reaching the peak of the mountain, Abraham builds an altar and is ready to sacrifice his

---

[4]Genesis 22:1–19.

beloved Isaac. Only an angel's voice crying out from heaven stops him from killing his son. God proclaims to Abraham that He is now sure of his faith and trust in God, and there is no need for him to kill his son.

According to the Midrash, Isaac, who was already a grown man, voluntarily went along with his father and was willing to be sacrificed.[5] Indeed, as Abraham raised his hand with the knife in it to kill him, Isaac, out of sheer fear, died. His soul left him and later returned to him. In willingly submitting to the will of God, Isaac shed his earthly existence. He died. And only by putting himself in the hands of God, that is, by subsuming himself to the will of God, did he rise again. That is why the Midrash tells us that at Mount Moriah Isaac's soul left him and then returned to him. In other words, Isaac experienced death and resurrection at Mount Moriah.[6]

We may ask what purpose there was in this trying and most difficult test which God put Abraham through, and what goal the death and revival of Isaac achieved. The Torah itself provides us with the answer to the first part of the question. Abraham was tested to show that he had absolute faith in God. This was a test to prove a point of reality itself, namely, that man is capable of totally subjugating his will to that of God's will, and of acting in

---

[5]Midrash Ham'vu'ar, Sefer Bresheet, pt. 2, (Jerusalem: Machon HaMidrash Ham'vu'ar, 1986), p. 548.

[6]Rabbaynu Shimon Hadarshan, *Yalkut Shimoni*, Jerusalem, 1960, p. 59. Rabbi Yehudah says, "When the sword reached [Isaac's] throat, his soul left him. But when he heard God's voice proclaiming between the two Cherubim 'Do not lay your hand upon the lad,' his soul returned to his body and revived him. At this point Isaac stood up and knew that this will be the way in which the dead will be revived in the future and he said 'Blessed art thou, Oh Lord our God who revives the dead."

total harmony with the Divine.[7] It was done in order to establish a fact about the nature of humankind, and to make it clear that man can obey the will of God in the same way that the physical universe did when it came into being at God's command. Just as the creation of the world came into being at God's command, so Abraham acted at the behest of God's command. That is, it shows us how much it was in the nature of Abraham to act in synchronization with the will of God. God's will and Abraham's will were one and the same. Instead of finding his own self by being in a state of confrontation with God, Abraham found his true self-realization and fulfilment by being in harmony with God and identifying his will with that of God's will. Therefore, Abraham was, indeed, the ultimate confidant of God.

Abraham's readiness to sacrifice his son is also an act of martyrdom. To subjugate one's love for a son to the love of one's God, and to even go beyond it and be willing to kill him in order to obey one's God, requires supernatural powers of self-sacrifice, emotional self-control, mental coolness, physical strength, courage and ultimate self-denial. Abraham was able to do all of these things at one and the same time because he was one with God. Isaac was similarly able to offer himself as a sacrifice to God, because he, too, like his father, was one with God. That was the ultimate test of Abraham's faith, that is, to show that he really walked before God. He, as well as Isaac, passed the test without equivocation. It is perhaps in this sense that we can best understand what God meant when he said of Abraham, "For I have known him, to the end that he may command his children and his household after him, that they may keep the way of the

---

[7]The sages state in the *Sayings of the Fathers,* "Make your will to be like His will so that His will shall be like your will." In other words the ultimate goal of man is to identify with the will of God. This is not to be confused with the concept of *Imitacio Dei.*

Lord, to do righteousness and justice; to the end that the Lord may bring upon Abraham that which He has spoken of him."[8]

However, it cannot be said that Abraham was a martyr in the full sense of the word.[9] The same can also be said of Isaac's death and resurrection, because neither Abraham nor Isaac committed their act of commitment to God in public view, they did it in the confines of their own and God's presence only. Only in the course of history did it become an act to be emulated by countless other people. In this sense, however, it can be regarded as an act of martyrdom.

Another act of martyrdom on the part of the Jewish people may bring us closer to our perception of what constitutes real martyrdom and provide us with a model for the martyrdom of the Holocaust.

That event is the theophany at Mount Sinai. The Midrash relates that when the Jewish people stood at Mount Sinai and heard God's voice they were overcome by the awesome power of the Almighty and "their souls left them . . . but the Torah interceded in their behalf and begged for God's compassion . . . and their souls were immediately restored to them."[10]

---

[8]Genesis 18:19.

[9]Even though the Yalkut Shimoni, op. cit., states that God regarded Abraham's readiness to sacrifice Isaac as though he were ready to sacrifice himself.

[10]Midrash Rabbah Ham'vuar on Sh'mot part II. (Jerusalem: Machon HaMidrash Ham'vuar, 1992), p. 40–41. Rabbi Levi said, "Israel asked for two things from the Holy One, blessed be He, that they should see His glory and hear His voice. And they saw His glory and they heard His voice, for it is said, 'and you said behold the Lord our God has shown us His glory and His might' (Deuteronomy 4:21) and it is also written (ibid.) 'and we heard His voice from within the midst of the fire' [when this took place they had no strength to stand for when they came to Sinai and God revealed Himself to them, their souls left them because He spoke to

According to the Midrash inherent in the argument of the Torah was the claim that the entire world was aware of the fact that the Jews were receiving the Torah at Mount Sinai. How else can one explain the argument that the Torah made in their behalf when it said, "The entire world will be rejoicing when it will see that your children are dying?"[11] Thus we are told that the encounter between the children of Israel and God was in the presence of the entire world.

Indeed, at Mount Sinai we have the ultimate example of what it means to be a martyr and what it takes to be one, not only for an individual but for an entire nation. The event at Mount Sinai meets all the criteria required of martyrdom: (1) It was a public act; (2) the martyrs in question had a choice to make. (They did not have to ask to see God's Glory and hear His voice.) However, they chose to do so even at the risk of their lives. In other words, the Jews would rather die with God than live without Him. In seeing God, the Jews became Jews even at the risk of their lives. They could not live without seeing God and still remain Jews any more than the Assarah Harugay Malchut could live as Jews without studying the Torah; (3) and this act of Jewish national martyrdom can be emulated. Indeed, the Midrash alludes to this issue when it states that Rabbi Levi said, "Is it possible that God did not know that if He lets the Jews see His Glory and hear His voice that they will not be able to with-

---

them as it is said (Song of Songs 5:6), 'My soul left me when He spoke.] But the Torah pleaded in their behalf before the Holy One, blessed be He, that He should have compassion upon them. It said 'Is there such a King who would marry off his daughter and at the same time kill all the members of his household? The entire world will rejoice when it will see that your children are dying! Immediately their souls were restored to them, as it is said, (Psalms 19:8) 'The Torah of the Lord is pure it restores the soul.'"
[11]Ibid.

---

stand it?" However, the Holy One, blessed be His Name, saw that in the future the Jews would create an idol, and in order they should not be able to say, "If God would have shown us His Glory and His Greatness and enabled us to hear His voice, we would not have created the idol." Therefore it is said, "Listen, Oh My people, and I will speak" (Psalms 81:9).[12] The Jews, therefore, have no excuse for building the golden calf and turning to paganism. However, all people, not only the Jews, can give up paganism and become monotheists. Indeed, not only can this act be emulated, it is worthy of imitation! The Jews were shown by God that when they identify with Him, they do not die but live. That applies to all the nations of the world. The Jews have shown that an entire nation can face God and live. Like the Jews, the nations of the world have no excuse for their pagan ways and rejection of God. This may be the reason that the rabbis also make a play on the word *Sinai*—the name of the mountain—and read it as *Sinah* (hatred). They say that the hatred of the Jews on the part of the nations of the world came down from Mount Sinai. At Mount Sinai the Jewish people received both life and death. They came away from the mountain with a lease on life and a threat of death. The rabbis have expressed this phenomenon, as they are wont to do, most succinctly when they said, "The sword and the scriptures came down bound together with each other from Heaven." Rabbi Eliezer tells us that God said to the Jews, "If you will keep the instructions that are written in the scriptures, then you will be saved from the sword,

---

[12]Midrash Rabbah, op. cit. The actual ninth verse of Psalm 81 is "Hear Oh my people and I will testify against you, Oh Israel if only you would listen to me." The Midrash interprets the verse thus, "Hear Oh my people and I will speak [that is, That I am your God] Oh Israel and I will testify against you [if you create idols]. Oh, if only you would listen to me [and not worship idols]." See commentary on the same in the Midrash.

and if not you will be smitten by it."[13] In other words, Jewish survival and Jewish destruction are bound up in Jewish attachment to the teachings of Mount Sinai. Thus we might say that in the presence of God at Mount Sinai the Jews died, but their acceptance of the Torah resurrected them. Indeed, the rabbis base this interpretation on the verse, "So, [God], expelled Adam [from the Garden of Eden], and He placed east of the garden of Eden the Cherubim, and the flaming sword that was ever turning [in all directions] in order to guard the way to the Tree of Life."[14] The Midrash discusses this verse in the context of Jewish suffering and Jewish prosperity. It concludes that while "Adam was commanded 'to guard the way to the Tree of life' he was not entrusted with the Tree of Life." The Torah, which is called "The Tree of Life," was given exclusively to the Jewish people. Hence the Jews can exist only, nay indeed can attain life everlasting only, by keeping the Torah.[15] Thus the theophany at Mount Sinai was the ultimate Jewish sacrifice and paradoxically also the penultimate resurrection. Just because they were willing to die for the privilege of beholding God's presence, God rewarded them with the gift of the Torah and life everlasting.

Many years after the Jewish people stood at Mount Sinai, the Prophet Ezekiel proclaimed to the children of Israel, "And I gave them My ordinances, and My judgements I made known to them, which if a man performs them he shall live through them. . . . But the Family of Israel rebelled against Me in the wilderness; in My decrees, they did not walk, and My ordinances

---

[13]Sifri, *D'varim* 11:12, *Torah im Malbim, Dvarim*, Israel, p. 123. The Midrash, see note 11, the expression ". . . if not you will be killed by the sword."

[14]Genesis 3:24. My translation.

[15]Midrash Ham'vu'ar, *Va'yikrah* pt. 2 (Jerusalem: Machon HaMidrash Ham'vuar, 1993), p. 420–421. See the footnotes to section six.

---

they spurned, which if a man performs them he shall live through them. . . .[16] The question is: "What does the Prophet Ezekiel mean by the statement, '. . . he shall live through them?' The *Metzudath David Commentary* tells us that it means that the ". . . ordinances and the judgements will vouchsave to the person who keeps them life in this world and in the world to come."[17] At first glance it would seem that the *Metzudath David* is telling us that the performance of the *mitzvot* will enable us to achieve eternal life. However, it looks as though he is making a distinction between life in this world and life in the next world, implying that the performance of the *mitzvot* will lead to a wholesome life in this world only and then in the world to come, but not eternal life in this world. The Radak[18] commenting on the same passage says that these words mean that one who keeps the *mitzvot* will live through them *Lichayay Almah*—eternal life. He relies on the Targum Onkelos of the same verse here and in Leviticus 18:5 that means that the performance of the *mitzvot* leads to life eternal.

Rashi, however, is more skeptical of this point of view. When he comments on the verse, "And you shall keep My ordinances and My judgements which if a man performs them he shall live through them,"[19] he says that the words "he shall live through them" means "In the world to come. But should anyone say that they refer to life eternity in this world, we will reply that it is impossible because we see that at the end people

---

[16]Ezekiel 20:11, 13. Artscroll Tanach Series. Edited by Rabbis Nosson Scherman and Meir Zlotowiz. Messorah Publications, Ltd., 1977.

[17]*Metzudath David Commentary on Ezekiel*, Mikra'oth G'doloth, part 9 (New York: Pardes Publishing House, Inc., 1951), p. 28.

[18]Radak, ibid.

[19]Leviticus, *Mikra'oth G'doloth*, pt. 4 (New York: Pardes Publishing House, Inc., 1951), p. 46b.

die."[20] Thus Rashi sees the performance of the *mitzvot* as a means of attaining life everlasting in the hereafter but not in this world. Consequently, it would be difficult to say, according to Rashi, that the Children of Israel attained eternal life at the time when they stood at Mount Sinai.

The Ramban, however, provides us with more information on this subject. After discussing this verse and its application to the amelioration of the social and civic order in this world, he tells us that there are different categories of people who keep the *mitzvot*.[21] The ultimate category of people who keep the *mitzvot* are:

> those people who forsake all matters pertaining to life in this world and do not pay any attention to it as though they did not have any physical body at all. Their entire purpose and goal in life is to be with their creator alone. As the case was with Elijah. When the souls of these people unite with the Glorious Name they live forever both in body and soul. This we see from what is written in Scripture about Elijah as well as what we know about him from the Kabbalah as well as what is said in the Midrashim about Chanoch and all the people from the Hereafter who are resurrected.[22]

---

[20]Ibid.

[21]Ibid.

[22]Ibid., verse 4. The Ramban concludes this passage with, "Therefore Scripture states with regards to the reward for the performance of the *mitzvot*: 'in order that you shall prolong your days,' Exodus 20:12), 'in order that you shall live' (Deuteronomy 30:19) 'and prolong your days' (Deuteronomy 22:7) because this form of speech contains within it all the categories of life. These words describe each category of mitzvah according to the merits of the people who observe them. Ramban enumerates that the other categories of people who keep the *mitzvot* are: People who do not keep the *mitzvot* for their own sake but do so in order to be

---

In Deuteronomy 5:23, in which the children of Israel say that nobody saw God speak and survived, the Ramban also says "Whoever hears the voice of God, Who is the source of life, will have his soul attach itself to and unite with its source. Such a person will no longer live the life of an ordinary mortal.[23]

Ibn Ezra, when commenting on verse 4 of Leviticus 18 also says, "The reason why God says to the the Jewish people, "Keep My ordinances and My judgements" is to explain to them that the ordinances and the judgements give life, both in this world and in the world to come, to those people who keep them. For whoever understands the secret of these laws will be kept alive by the One Who Lives Eternally. Such a person will never die."[24]

Thus, we see that eternal life in this world is in fact real and attainable by people who would reach out for it. The children of Israel who stood at Mount Sinai reached out for it when they clamored to see God. At that time they attained eternal life.

It is worth citing what the Zohar has to say about this matter:

Rabbi Judah said in the name of Rabbi Chiya, in the name of Rabbi Jose: "When the Israelites heard the words of the Holy One, their souls flew from them and ascended to the Throne of Glory in order to cleave to it." Said the Torah to the Holy One: "Was it for nothing and to no purpose that

rewarded will indeed be rewarded with material wealth in this world; People who keep the *mitzvot* in order to live in the hereafter do so out of fear. They will escape the punishment of the wicked in the hereafter; People who keep the *mitzvot* properly out of love and fear of God. Such people will be rewarded with a good life in this world and with life in the hereafter.

[23]Ramban. *D'varim, Mikra'ot G'dolot*. (New York: Pardes Publishing House Inc., 1951), p. 17b.
[24]Ibn Ezra, Leviticus, op. cit.

I was fashioned two thousand years before the creation of the world? Is it all in vain that in me is inscribed "Every man of the children of Israel and of the strangers that sojourn among them" (Leviticus 17:13), "speak to the children of Israel" (Leviticus 24:15), "the children of Israel are servants unto me" (Leviticus 25:55). "These are the children of Israel," and diverse many other words of like character?' Where, then, are these children of Israel? At that hour the children of Israel received again the souls which fled in the wake of the Divine splendor, for the Torah returned them every one to its own place: yea she took hold of them and gave them back to their owners, each to the body which was its proper dwelling. This is the significance of the words: "The Torah of the Lord is perfect, *returning (meshibath)* the soul (Psalms 29:7): 'returning' in the literal sense."[25]

It is clear that the *Zohar* links the resurrection of the Jewish people with the intercession of the Torah on their behalf. But at the same time it also states that even though Moses tried to prepare them for the awesome fright that they would experience at the moment of the encounter with God, they were not prepared for it. Consequently when the moment of truth arrived, their souls left them.[26] How aptly this describes the history of Jewish martyrdom! No matter how much the Jews have girded themselves in the course of time to give their lives for the sake of their God, Torah and people, they always came away from it weakened and diminished. Only the love of the Torah revived them and restored them to their glory as God's children.

[25]Harry Sperling, Maurice Simon, and Dr. Paul P. Levertoff, trans. *The Zohar*, vol. 3 (London and New York: The Soncino Press, 1984), p. 256–257.
[26]Ibid.

However, the *Zohar* goes beyond the death and resurrection of the Jews. According to this passage of the *Zohar*, not only do the Jews exist because of the Torah, but the Torah can exist only because of the Jews. God, who created the world by the words of the Torah, must have the Jews in order to give purpose and meaning to the Torah and preserve the world.[27] Thus when Jews are martyred for the sake of God and the Torah, and resurrected, it is in order to preserve the very existence of the world. That makes it impossible for the Jews to perish if the world is to continue to exist, because the Jews preserve the Torah and without the Torah, the world cannot exist.

The Talmud[28] tells us that Rabbi Joshua ben Levy said: "At every word that came out of the mouth of the Holy One, blessed be He, the souls of the Israelites left, departed from them, as it is said, 'My soul departed when He spoke.' (Song of Songs 5:6). But, asks the Gemarah, if their souls departed at the first word, how could they receive the second word? God brought down the dew with which He will resurrect the dead[29] and He revived them, as it is said, 'You Oh, God sent a generous rain, You did confirm Your inheritance, when it was weary.'" (Psalms 68:10)

According to Rashi, *Shabbath* 88b, with the word *dew* the Psalmist refers to the words of the Torah. Thus we are again informed that it was the Torah that resurrected the Jewish people at Mount Sinai. Even though the Jews died each time they heard God's word, they were resurrected by the words of the Torah time and again. Torah, Jewish martyrdom and resurrection are inalienably intertwined.

---

[27]The commentary on the *Zohar* (Matok Midvash, Sefer Zohar HaKadosh im perush Matok Midvash, pt. 6 (Jerusalem: Machon Da'at Yoseph, 1994), p. 193 states, "If the Jews would not have been revived the law would not have been engraved upon the Tablets because without the Jewish people the Torah was also dead."
[28]*Shabbath* 88b. (Vilna: The Widow and Brothers Romm, 1920).
[29]*Chagiga* 12b. (Vilna: The Widow and Brothers Romm, 1920).

In discussing the subject of the nature and behavior of the Jewish people at Mount Sinai, Rabbi Joshua ben Levy tells us that when the Jews heard the words of God at Mount Sinai, they not only died but also retreated from the mountain twelve mil. However, the ministering angels forced them to come back.[30] Rabbi Yehoshuah ben Levy also informs us that at the time when God spoke, with each word that he uttered, the whole world was filled with the fragrance of spices that were carried off by the wind that God especially created for that purpose, and placed in the Garden of Eden to be used for the future resurrection of the souls.[31]

The MaHarshah[32] points out that there is a contradiction in what Rabbi Yehoshuah ben Levy says. Firstly, if the Jews retreated twelve mil with each word that they heard of God, how could they have died? Secondly, if the world was filled with fragrance to revive them, again, how could they have died?

The MaHarshah explains these seeming contradictions this way. He says that the Jewish people were divided into three groups based upon their natural characteristics. The first group consisted of those people who were physically weak. When they heard the great sound of the Heavenly Voice of God, they became very weak. For this group, the fragrance of the spices was created in order to help them regain their strength. The second group was even weaker. The people of this group died. They were resurrected. The third group of people apparently was stronger. The people of this group retreated twelve mil with each word that they heard coming from God. These people were pushed back to the mountain by the angels.

---

[30] *Shabbath*, op. cit.
[31] Ibid., Chidushay Halachoth V'Haggadoth, MaHarshah on *Shabbath, ibid.*, back of Gemarah, p. 25a.
[32] Ibid.

The MaHarshah further states[33] that instead of asking Rabbi Yehoshuah ben Levy "if the Jews died when they heard the first word come from God, how did they accept the second word?" they should have asked, "How did they come to life for the second word?" He explains this dilemma by interpreting the meaning of the passages from the psalm upon which this passage of the Talmud is based.

He says that the Gemarah is telling us something especially new, that is, that the Jews died every time they heard God's word, and that they died and were resurrected ten times. This the rabbis deduce from the fact that the psalmist says, in conjunction with the resurrection of the Jewish people that took place at Mount Sinai, *geshem nidavot*, the word *nidavot* is plural. Therefore, it should be translated as "continuous bountiful rain." It is also written in the same psalm, "The earth quaked . . . this is Sinai".[34] Consequently, the MaHarshah concludes that the Jews died from all the noise and quaking of the earth that took place at Mount Sinai, and then the "continuous bountiful rain" came and resurrected them. He also points out that Scripture calls dew, *tal*, that is, "continuous bountiful rain," because dew never ceases to exist, but rain comes only as a gift of God and an act of Divine mercy when mankind merits it.

---

[33]Ibid.

[34]Psalms 68:8–10: "O God, when you went forth before Your nation, When You marched through the wilderness, Selah: The earth roared, even the heavens dropped before the presence of God, This is Sinai before the presence of God, the God of Israel. A generous rain did you Lavish, O God, When your heritage was weary You established it firmly." The translation of the psalms are from the *Tehilim*, vol. 3, Artscroll Tanach Series, commentary and trans. by Rabbi Avrohom Chaim Feuer in collaboration with Rabbi Nosson Scherman (Brooklyn, NY: Mesorah Publications, Ltd., 1979), pp. 831–833.

We can now return to the subject of the martyrdom of the Jewish people at Mount Sinai. According to the MaHarshah's interpretation of Rabbi Yehoshuah ben Levy's words, we can see that when the Jewish people stood at the foot of Mount Sinai, before God appeared on the Mountain and spoke to them, they proclaimed in unison to Moses that they would do everything that God will tell them, as we are told in the words of the Torah, "And the entire nation answered in one voice and said, everything that God said we shall do."[35] However, when He actually spoke to them, they quickly found out that they could not tolerate the awesome power of God's voice. Some tried to avoid listening to it by running away; some just could not take it and fainted, and others died listening to it. No one could remain unscathed in the presence of the Divine. The only question that remains for those who would stand in the presence of God is, "How they will face God? Will they run away from the face of God? Will they collapse and die? Will they faint into oblivion?"

Those who run from the presence of God may be physically stronger than those who do not, as the MaHarshah tells us, but spiritually they are weaker. When they run, they actually try to deny the existence of God. They cannot face the reality of their own weakness and dependence on God. They cannot accept the reality that they cannot escape the presence of God. In spite of the fact that they can never behold the face of God, they must nevertheless resign themselves to serve Him like a servant who brings the food to his master's table, but can never look him straight in the eye. Those who are weak and faint in the presence of God are both physically and mentally exhausted by the ordeal

---

[35]Exodus 19:8. The Ramban points out that this verse and Exodus 24:7, "Everything that God has said we will do and we will listen," were said by the people to Moses before God appeared on Mount Sinai.

of confronting the challenge of the presence of God and what it means to constantly bear the yoke of the Heavenly kingdom upon their shoulders. They become worn out, and fatigue takes over their lives in the course of time. These are the people who cannot bear the constant awareness of standing in the presence of God. They collapse under the pressure and weight that God's laws place on them. Those who die are the people who are resolute to the last breath. These people will for the sake of standing in the presence of God and behold His Glory give their last breath. These are the people who are the real martyrs of the faith.

The events at Mount Sinai were a mirror image of all the Jewish history that was to follow. It is a paradigm of the tragedy of the *Shoah* of our time as well. The martyrdom of the Jews at Mount Sinai who died because they wanted to face God is the one and only model of Jewish martyrdom for all times and especially for the unique self-sacrifice of those who died in the *Shoah*.

During the *Shoah* there were also those Jews who in the face of annihilation tried to run away from God and the Jewish people. They sought succor in the strange world that did not want them in the first place. These are the Jews who turned to atheism, communism, socialism, and even secular Zionism, not to mention the various avant guard movements, in order to lose themselves in the sea of humanity, in the false hope that they would save themselves from death at the hands of the Nazi machine. We now know that few such Jews survived. As the Jews who tried to escape the theophany at Mount Sinai by moving away from the mountain were pushed back by the angels to face their maker at the mountain, so were those who tried to escape the *Shoah* betrayed, killed and rejected by their would-be saviors.[36] These Jews, like the Jews at Mount Sinai, could not face

---

[36]That is not to say that there were no individuals who even at the risk of their own lives did not try to save some Jews. There were

the reality that only in the presence of God do they have real life. They showed that they were only too human and could not face God. Their would-be savior angels turned into angels of death. The political movements and the intellectual currents of the age that enticed them also in the end devoured them. There is hardly a trace left of them as there is no trace left of the Jews of the Sinai generation and all the generations that followed them who tried to find life in the arms of alien gods and strange ways of life.

The Jews who came out of the *Shoah* mentally broken, spiritually exhausted, and physically collapsed are like the Jews who in the presence of God at Mount Sinai fainted. The ordeal of facing God was too much for them, just as the inferno of the *Shoah* that was consuming the world was too difficult and awesome a challenge for these Jews. They came out of the *Shoah* spent of all life. Only the miracle of the fragrance of the Divine spices, the spirit of the word of the Torah, could, and did, bring them back to life. These are the Jews who, after the *Shoah*, rebuilt and renewed the Jewish institutions of learning around the world and thus resurrected the Jewish people.

The Jews who died during the *Shoah*, however, were the real martyrs. Like the Jews at Mount Sinai who died in the presence of God, they too looked death in the eye and died a noble death, in the knowledge that they were dying because they are Jews. In their death, they faced God and embraced Him with their last ounce of strength, while returning their souls to Him Who gave it to them in the first place. They went to their death knowing full well why they were being killed, just as the Jews at the foot of Mount Sinai knew what was going to happen to them if they remained standing there.

After the *Shoah* a blasphemous notion was let loose in the

---

such noble souls. But they were very few in number and are rare exceptions.

---

world that the Jews went to their death like sheep to the slaughter. What a lie! What a prevarication of history! What a perversion of the truth!

The Jews went to their death with dignity and with pride! They knew they were going to be killed. They went quietly and with solemnity. I know. I was there. I was led together with my mother, sisters, brother and relatives. We all knew that we were about to be killed. Nobody panicked. Nobody blasphemed against God. We walked, resigned, to face our destiny in the presence of God. I recall the march from the Ghetto to the outskirts of our town. Surrounded by Belarussian, Estonian, German, Latvian, Lithuanian, Polish and Ukrainian militia serving with the Germans, we marched to our death. We marched quietly, solemnly, fearful and frightened. Many prayed. Many wept. But we walked straight. We walked as Jews. We walked with faith in God to the last moment. Only by a miracle were some of us saved. Those who did not return from the last march knew why they did not. They knew that they gave their last breath because they were Jews and nothing else. Their martyrdom was real Jewish martyrdom.

Like Isaac at the beginning of time, like the brothers of Lod, the Assarah Harugay Malchuth, the Jews in the age of the crusades, and the martyrs of York and the massacres of 1648, they died because they were Jews. But most of all they died as the Jews at Mount Sinai did, for the pure reason of affirming their faith in the One and Only God, the God of our forefathers and mothers, the God of Mount Sinai, the God of Abraham, Isaac and Jacob, Sarah, Rebecca, Rachel and Leah, Creator of Heaven and earth! They did not die for the sake of a better humanity! They did not die for the sake of the amelioration of the lot of man! They did not die to improve the social conditions of one group or another. They died for the Torah, God and the Jewish people.

Among those whom I lost on that fateful day in addition to

my mother, Bashkeh, of blessed memory, was my infant brother, who was only five or six months old. He was born soon after my father, Dovid, of blessed memory, was killed. Every time I read or hear that the Holocaust was not in vain because it teaches humanity about the need to be good and nice to each other, the image of my mother holding my brother in her arms, tears rolling down her cheeks, telling me to cry so that God will save me, comes to my mind. My body shudders and my blood boils. No, they did not die for some now politically correct cause! No! How dare they exploit their death for social action!! No, they did not die for humanity! They died for God! They died for the Torah! They died for the Jewish people!

How dare they, who have created a cult of the Holocaust, pervert the death of my mother, father, and baby brother and the millions of *Shoah* martyrs to suit their agenda of political correctness and commercialization? Have they asked those who died why they died and for whom they died? By whose leave are they doing this? No and once more no! The *Shoah* can serve only one cause. It must remind us why we are Jews! Just as the death of those who stood at Mount Sinai reminds us why they were there. Nothing else![37]

—CR

---

[37]Interestingly enough, just as the Jews built a golden calf right after the theophany at Mount Sinai, the Jews soon after the *Shoah* turned to all kinds of contemporary idols in the disguise of various political, social and intellectual movements. But just as the worshippers of the golden calf did not survive, so too do we see the disintegration and collapse of the secular movements. But the religious and Torah-true world is being revived and rebuilt both in Israel and in exile.

20

The Threefold Nature
of Jewish Resistance
in the Days of the *Shoah*

The nature and grandeur of Jewish resistance during the *Shoah* is neither properly understood nor appreciated because people do not know or want to know the circumstances under which, and the values by which, the Jewish people lived. Jewish resistance during the *Shoah* consisted of one, a denial of reality, two, physical resistance, and, three, moral resistance.

DENIAL OF REALITY

The Jewish people did not accept the fact that the Germans were literally out to exterminate them root and branch. They treated the threat of the Germans to kill them, put them in ghettos, concentration camps, confiscate their property and ban them from society as a passing phase that would soon go away with the change of the government in Berlin, through the intervention of the western and even the communist powers, and the general outcry of humanity. Jews were used to persecution and oppression as well as to extortion and pogroms. After all, the anti-Semitic outcry *Hep! Hep!* originated in Germany. One more set back in the long history of their ongoing struggle for emancipation and equal rights as citizens of the lands of their sojournment for thousands of years was not unusual. Furthermore, the enormity of the crime was beyond belief and imagination. The Jewish people could not conceptualize it and therefore they also could not believe nor accept the fact that such a monstrous design was possible. The Jews could neither believe nor imagine the fact that Germany into which, over the last hundred years, their sons flocked from Eastern Europe to study and become modernized, would do such a thing. The Jews looked up to Germany as the land of culture, civilization and science. It was in their eyes the most advanced country in Europe, if not in the world. They looked upon it as the land of Goethe, Kant, Schiller, Lessing and other great men of letters, and Nobel prize winners. Such a land could never perpetrate the crimes plotted by the Nazis. It must also be added that many Jews in Eastern Europe had memories of Germany from World War II when they regarded the Germans as saviors compared to the Russians and the communists. One must also add the fact that the Germans did not attack the Jews suddenly and at one time. They attacked the Jews in stages, gradually and in different ways so as to create the impression that it was temporary and necessary to help the war effort.

I can bear personal witness to these observations.

I remember as a child in my home town of Zdienciol. (Zshettel), in the province of Grodna, Poland (now Belarus) how people were talking with my parents, of blessed memory, about the refugees who came from those parts of Poland that were occupied by Germany in 1939. They were saying the Germans were forcing the Jews into special parts (ghettos) of the big cities, and they did not know what was going to happen to the Jewish people there. My parents, of blessed memory, were equally unsure of what was going to happen to themselves as well as the refugees, now that we were all under the Russian occupation, since our part of Poland was occupied by Russia in 1939. It seemed to me that they were just as anxious and disturbed whether they spoke about the Germans or the Russians. I could feel a sense of uncertainty and worry, but not a sense of doom. I heard it being said that the Germans were bad to the Jews, but not that they were killing them. Yet that was the time when the Germans and their collaborators were already laying the foundation for the extermination of the Jewish people. Yes, the Jews could not accept such a new version of reality!

I remember that in 1941 when the Germans occupied our part of Poland after declaring war on Russia, our neighbor across the street from our house, in whose orchard I used to play with my friends who lived near me, saying "Thank God the Germans have come. Now we are rid of the communists." He was still thinking of the Germans in terms of World War I. Little did he know that the day would come when he would have to pray for the return of the communists. I remember this story well because it was repeated many times during the following days of blood and death that continuously plagued us for the rest of the war, from which out of a community of nearly five thousand Jews, only some one hundred and fifty survived. My neighbor across the street was one of the first to die. Yes the Jews could not accept the fact that the Germans were out to murder them!

I remember well how Jews who escaped the murder of the Jewish people in their towns came to our town and told us how the entire Jewish populations of their towns were exterminated in one day, and how the local gentile neighbors participated in the blood bath. But we did not believe them and their stories. We said that they must have done something to provoke the Germans, their gentile population has a reputation for being anti-semitic, it would never happen here. We had good neighbors, our German police are better. We had many make-believe excuses not to accept the dark reality looming above our heads. Yes, we were resisting the reality of the Germans by resisting the bitter reality that awaited all of us!

PHYSICAL RESISTANCE

The resistance of the Jewish people to the Nazis was unlike any other resistance in the course of a people's struggle for either survival and dignity or national independence and pride, in the annals of human history. When nations struggle for survival or independence, they are usually occupied by a foreign power on the one hand, and have the tacit, if not the active, support of the indigenous population on the other. That is, those people from within the native population who choose to rise up in arms to fight the occupying power have the depth of their country and native population to turn to for support, to retreat to when necessary, or as a source of manpower. In other words, the fighting elements of the nation struggling for independence and freedom have a friendly population to turn to. That is the normal and, one might even say, routine nature of armed struggle for national independence and survival.

That was not the lot of the Jewish people fighting to survive! Not only did the local population not support the Jews in their struggle against the Germans and their collaborators, but they also turned against the Jewish people and often outdid the Nazis in their vicious murder of Jews. Though there were some individual people who came to the help of the Jews, the overwhelming majority of native people joined the Germans in the killing of the Jews. So the Jews had to fight not only the Germans but also, and often with greater difficulty, the native population, the nextdoor neighbor, the fellow professional, the farmer, the merchant, the customer, the playmate and school friend, now turned informer, the robber, the murderer and the enemy who was worse than the German. Under such circumstances the question is not why the Jews didn't resist, but how could they resist at all? Yet resist they did.

The Jewish people fought the Germans and their collaborators every step of the way. I will speak only of my own memories. In my own small town we organized a resistance group in the ghetto. The Judenratt refused to give the Germans a list of the old and children, and they escaped from the ghetto into the forest to organize a partisan group. After our ghetto was exterminated, the Jews who managed to save themselves and escape to the forest known as Lipitchanskaya Pushtcha, organized a fighting group of young men and women who tried to fight the Germans. Between August 1943 and December 1943 there was a group, an armed force of over three hundred men and women under arms, who fought the Germans. This fighting force was virtually decimated when the Germans brought in an army of some thirty thousand soldiers, who attacked the forests in our region of Belarus in order to eliminate the danger of the partisans to the German armies on their march to Russia. The partisans were no match for the German army. As a result of this German offensive, the Jewish Brigade was disbanded and the Jewish partisans who survived joined the Russian groups that operated behind the German lines in our region of Belarus.

The Jewish partisans had many problems to overcome in addition to the confrontation with the Germans. I will list just a few of them.

Perhaps the most pervasive problem was the constant need for secrecy and cover in order to avoid being discovered by the local population. To be merely noticed by a shepherd, a farmer or a woodsman meant certain attack by the Germans and their militia, because the local people were most certain to inform against us. Thus even in the forest out of sight of the Germans, we had to be constantly on guard. There was never any rest. We were always on the move and stayed no more than about two or three weeks in any given place. This need to be constantly on the move was especially difficult in the winter time.

Food was another problem. We went hungry for many a month and many people died from starvation. Often the food we obtained was taken by force from some farmers. Some of the time it was given by good peasants and most often it was obtained by intercepting convoys of farmers taking their provisions as annual tributes to the German garrisons in the nearby towns. However, that was a risky undertaking because these convoys were accompanied by German guards.

Another problem was that we were perpetually exposed to attacks by the Germans and their militia. We had to be always on guard. There were many raids on our camps and many of us died during such attacks upon our camps.

Perhaps the most difficult problem we had was the lack of weapons, because without weapons, we were totally defenseless and vulnerable to all and any attack from all and any source. How indeed did we obtain weapons? The first weapons that I remember the Jewish partisans obtained were those purchased from some peasants in exchange for a jacket and some pants. The Jewish partisans gave the peasant clothing in exchange for a rifle, some bullets and an old pair of pants and a shirt. The Jewish man literally gave the peasant the shirt off his back. Some pistols and some rifles were bought for money. Some weapons were taken from the farmers by force of arms under the threat of death. We found out which farmers had weapons from their own neighbors, who would tell us either voluntarily or in response to requests that they should surrender their weapons. To show that they had no weapons of their own, and that they had good will toward the partisans, they would point out which farmers did harbor weapons. Their information was always correct. The Belarussian farmers had weapons because they picked them up from the dead Russian soldiers who were lying on the roadsides and in the fields. They were killed as they were running away from the advancing German armies. Their weapons, consisting of rifles, hand guns, machine guns and bullets, were strewn all over the fields and highways and by-ways waiting to be picked up, and indeed the farmers picked them up.

When the first few rifles were bought, the Jewish partisans went out on an ambush against a German patrol. It was a successful mission. I recall somehow the fact that the German patrol consisted of about four or five soldiers. They were attacked and killed. The Jewish partisans returned to the forest with new German rifles, some hand grenades, bullets and belts. We were all excited. We now had more rifles taken in combat. That took place one day in late August of 1943.

In the course of about three years, our partisans have attacked German military garrisons and patrols, blew up bridges, confiscated food transports, derailed and blew up military trains carrying soldiers or equipment, and carried out intelligence gathering missions, yes and also avenged the death of some of our martyrs by executing those farmers and townspeople who were known to have killed Jews and collaborated with the Germans. All of this was done not only behind the German lines, but also in the midst of a hostile civilian population and often in the face of the Polish National Army resistance groups that operated clandestinely in our parts of the forest. They attacked our Jewish groups, including the civilian Jewish camps in the forests, whenever they could. In fact they were posed as much a threat to our lives as the Germans did. The Jewish partisans had to fight a war simultaneously on two fronts. They had to fight the German enemy and the local hostile population at one and the same time with hardly any weapons or ammunition. To make up for the shortage of weapons they improvised. For example, mortar and artillery shells were converted into mines. Mines were improved so that once they were laid, they could not be disarmed because they were made to explode once put in place.

Our partisans died fighting the Germans and the Polish National Army, which usually ambushed our men. As far as I can remember, we never attacked them. Our partisans died fighting not only as members of the Russian armed struggle against the murdering German forces, but also as Jews who fought for the dignity of their people, and as Jews who wanted to avenge the death of their dearest relatives and loved ones even though they knew that they might never survive the war. Like Samson of old, they went into battle with the thought "Let me die together with my enemies."

MORAL RESISTANCE

One of the most amazing aspects of the *Shoah* is the fact that a most insignificant number, if any at all, of the Jews tried to convert to Christianity or tried to assume gentile identities in order to survive. The conventional explanation is that the Germans were killing any person who had one quarter of Jewish blood in his or her veins and therefore it was impossible for a Jew to escape by converting. This, however, is a very superficial explanation. In fact, Jews who wanted to hide as Christians could have done so. In the confusion of the mass movements of refugees and thousands of people who moved from their home towns to new places where nobody knew them, it would not have been too difficult for Jews to take on the identity of non-Jews. Indeed the Jews of Poland and the other Eastern European countries, not to mention the Western European countries, were very much integrated into their society and knew the language, customs and general manners of their country as well as any native. In fact, Jews who tried to pass as Christians usually succeeded.

The fact that the Jews did not try to convert is one of the most amazing aspects of the saga of the *Shoah.* It speaks volumes about the depth of the Jew's attachment to Judaism and the Jewish people.

In the course of the war, the Jews also showed that they could rise to great spiritual heights. They conducted religious services wherever and whenever possible, tried to keep the dietary laws of Kashruth, helped each other and maintained their faith in God and His ultimate redemption of the Jewish people. All of these things they did at a considerable risk to their lives and in the presence of overwhelming pressure to doubt and question the presence of God.

I remember how we tried to conduct a *mincha maariv* service as soon as we had a *minyan* of men with us in the forest. We had no prayer books but we had amongst us a father and two sons who were Meshorerim, and they knew the prayers by heart. The older one acted as the Shliach Tzibbur and the men gathered around him to pray and recite the kaddish. In retrospect I often think about this event. How strange and heroic this was. Here we were frightened, hungry, full of fear and sorrow, all of us just escaped with our lives, too shocked to even cry, uncertain of our next day or even hour, standing in the forest hungry and not knowing how to even survive the night, the sun about to set but still appearing through the tree tops, a slight dampness on the ground and we were gathering in prayer to praise God and to sanctify His glorious name in spite of and because of our parents, children, wives, husbands, brothers, and sisters who were killed. Our faith in God was never shaken and our way of life never daunted or questioned. We did what came naturally to us . We prayed. We praised God. We embraced the souls of our loved ones as they ascended to their heavenly abode to dwell in the presence of God amidst Abraham, Isaac, and

Jacob, and Sarah, Rebecca, Rachel and Leah, as well as all our saintly ancestors. That was the natural thing to do. Today when I hear people ask "Where was God during the *Shoah*?" I shake with anger. To me such talk is a profanation of the memories, the lives and deaths of all those martyrs who died with faith in their hearts and prayers on their lips, as well as all of us who never questioned our God and our Jewish way of life.

I remember how we were worried when Passover was approaching and we had no matzah. How could we face Passover without matzah? So, I remember that it was agreed that it would be all right to make thin patties out of meal made of groats, and that would do in place of the matzah in time of an emergency. We tried to keep the laws of Passover as much as possible. Unfortunately we did not have may options. We scarcely had potatoes and berries to eat and that was no problem as far as Passover was concerned. But engraved on my mind ever since then is the concern that the adults showed about the proper observance of *Pesach*. It was the natural thing to do. Jews must keep the Passover.

I remember that in the terrible days in the forest when we were starving from hunger and only had a piece of lard smaller than the size of a graham cracker per day, my aunt refused to eat it because it was lard and not kosher. We were freezing and starving to death. She would offer us, the little children, her portion. There were certain things that Jews could not eat because they were Jews, even at the point of hunger.

This is how ordinary Jews acted. They accepted life as it was. They never flinched from their steadfast commitment to their way of life. In their simple unassuming ways, they displayed an inner strength and faith unmatched by the pontificating of many a philosopher and theologian who use their martyrdom as a means of promoting their heretical notions. What I have seen and witnessed with my own eyes can be multiplied thousands of times in the accounts of Jewish martyrs and survivors of the

Shoah. There were Jews in every concentration camp, in every ghetto, in every forest and in every hiding place, who always kept faith with the heritage of the Jewish people.

In persevering in the observance of the ways of the Jewish people, in clinging steadfastly to the Jewish faith and rituals, the Jewish people displayed a nobility of spirit and the courage of resistance far greater than that of people who resort to the force of arms.

When the *Shoah* was on the dark horizon of history, the Jewish people could not accept its reality because of the enormity of its brutality and because they could not imagine that human beings would act like that. When, however, the Jews were confronted by the actuality of the *Shoah*, they took up arms and fought heroically whenever possible and always offered moral and spiritual resistance unsurpassed in the annals of human history.

—*CR*

21

Kristalnacht—Another Look

As matters have evolved in the writing of the history of the *Shoah, Kristalnacht* has emerged as a unique phenomenon, and will go down in the annals of history as the paramount event of the *Shoah* that preserved it as a special and sacred Jewish experience. The special Jewish character of almost every massacre of the Jewish people that took place during the dark days of the *Shoah* is being challenged as having been directed solely against the Jewish people. Instead these terrible events are being portrayed as acts of violence against other nationalities and religions as well, thereby taking away the cutting edge of the *Shoah* as a blight on the name of all religions and nations for allowing the

Germans to single out the Jewish people for slaughter and not coming to their aid. Now due to these revisions, it can be argued that not only the Jews but all people were being attacked by the Germans and therefore the Jews are not entitled to any special treatment.

Indeed it may be shown, and rightly so, that the Germans and their cohorts murdered many millions of people other than Jews. That, however, does not alter the fact that the *Shoah* was a uniquely Jewish event in history because the Germans did not have any other official state policy to exterminate any other religious group or people besides the Jews with the exception of the Gypsies and even they to had ways of escape that the Jews did not have. The millions of other nationals who were murdered, died because their country was at war, or they were caught up in the conflict between the Germans and their own country in one way or another. Not so the Jews. No matter what they did or did not do their fate was sealed. They were doomed to death. Anyone who wanted could and did kill them with perfect legal immunity. There was no law against killing a Jew. There were laws against the killing of any other human being. There were no Jewish armies marching to the goose steps of the Germans as there were armies of every other nation in Europe. Why then the desire and need to falsify history and pervert the nature of the *Shoah*?

A simple answer is of course the fact that the Allies may have removed Nazism from the world, but they have not removed anti-semitism. After the war the anti-Semites remained silent but not inactive. As soon as the heat of the war began to cool off, they and their collaborators began an insidious campaign to deny the *Shoah* and propagate the idea that it was a Jewish invention to malign the good name of the Germans and other good people of Europe. This lie, however, could not be maintained in the face of reality. In any case the open and obvious anti-Semites could not succeed because anti-semitism was politically incorrect following the war.

This reality was such that it called into question the moral authority of the Protestant church and, especially, the Roman Catholic Church. It is from this direction that the main thrust came for the dilution of the *Shoah* as a unique Jewish experience and a human tragedy of world proportion that proclaimed the moral and religious failure of the great Western religions, Catholicism and Protestantism. The *Shoah* was a powerful indictment of these religions for their silence, passivity and overall inaction in the face of the horrible German extermination of the Jewish people. It is no wonder that following World War II, the status of western religion declined, especially in the eyes of the young generations all over the world. To combat this and to save the credibility, the churches and some of the governments of the free world whose leaders had the decency to feel guilty for standing by and allowing the extermination of the Jews to proceed uninterrupted, came up with a three-pronged counter-offensive. This counteroffensive consisted of the classical stages of anti-semitism displayed over the ages starting with the inception of the Jewish people as a nation and a religion.

These stages are beautifully explained by the great Maimonides in his immortal epistle to the people of Yemen in the twelfth century known as Iggeret Taiman. Maimonides describes the phases of anti-semitism as following a chronological pattern, but there is no reason why they could not occur coevally at any stage of history. As it happens with regards to the *Shoah*, due to historical circumstances, and the need to compress the events into a short period of time, they appear to be taking place simultaneously. We will appreciate each stage better if we discuss them separately, the way Maimonides does.

The first stage in the attack on the Jewish people was paganism. This, in essence, is a denial of the validity of Judaism. The second stage was the age of Greek philosophy, which challenged the veracity and intellectual integrity of Judaism. The third stage was the rise of Christianity, which attempted to obfuscate the barriers between Judaism and itself, and thus confuse and befog the minds of the Jewish people by claiming that Christianity is the true Judaism and that the Judaism of the Jews is a false Judaism.

The same strategy was and is being applied to the question of the *Shoah* and the relationship of the Jewish people and the rest of the world to it. First comes the denial that it took place altogether. That is followed by the argument that it was not possible to help the Jews. It was too dangerous, the people and the world were not aware of what was going on, to help the Jews would have diverted from the national effort of the war etc., etc. Finally comes the argument that the Jewish people were not the only ones to have been murdered. Other nationals were also murdered, it is argued. Finally we have a scenario where it can be said that the Jews were merely "casualties of the war" and a monastery can be built on the grounds of Auschwitz. Before too long, the ground is laid for future generations to think that only Christians were persecuted by the Germans and that the Christians were the real heroes of the war because they fought and opposed the Nazi Antichrist.

Not so, however, with regards to the issue of *Kristalnacht*. No one can dare to say that other regions were equally persecuted as the Jews and that their religious institutions were also destroyed. *Kristalnacht* is a unique Jewish experience!

The German hordes rampaged through the streets of the cities of Germany and Austria on November 9, 1938, killing several hundred Jews, arresting and sending to concentration camps some thirty thousand people, demolishing 7,500 Jewish businesses and destroying 1,118 synagogues. No churches were destroyed that night. No Christian businesses were demolished that night. No Christians were killed that night. On that infamous night and day only the Jews were singled out for torture, murder, pillage, deportation, humiliation and expulsion from the human race. That "Night of Broken Glass" marked the beginning of the *Shoah*. That night will also serve as a monumental testament to all eternity that the *Shoah* can mean one thing alone, the attempt by Germany and its collaborating European nations to exterminate the Jewish people while the rest of the world and the great western religions stood by in silence! It shall forever remain a date of painful memory and sorrow to the Jewish people and a date of shame and guilt for the western world and Christianity!

—*CR*

22

Some Possible Lessons
for a Response to the Holocaust

Half a century after the *Shoah* we still ask the question, "Why?" While we may never come up with a wholly satisfying response, nevertheless we might distill from the profound personal heroism displayed by individual Jews, men and women alike, an answer to these difficult questions. The reaction of these heroes and heroines may not only give us an inkling of what they felt and thought about the tremendous pain, suffering and death they experienced, but also give us a picture of their attitude and perception of the meaning of life and death and the role of God in the ever unfolding drama of human suffering. In the end, this may help us to develop a better understanding of the meaning of the *Shoah*.

During the struggle for Israel's independence, the British executed a number of Freedom Fighters. Among them were Avshalom Chaviv, Yaakov Weiss and Meir Nekker. Prior to their execution and in the course of time before these heroes were put to death, they were approached by a number of people who tried to comfort them and talk with them about their impending death. In the course of these conversations, the question about the purpose and meaning of their life and death arose. Their comments cast a very sharp light on these topics and teach us volumes about their moral thinking about the meaning of life and death in the last days of their lives.

They told their visitors the story of Rabbi Akiva, who himself was the martyr par excellence during the Hadrianic persecution of the Jewish people in the first half of the second century of the common era, and the story of a Jewish mother during the expulsion of the Jewish people from Spain in 1492.

The story of Rabbi Akiva's death is as follows. Before he was tortured to death his disciples questioned the purpose and meaning of his sacrifice on behalf of Torah and Judaism. To this Rabbi Akiva responded by saying that all his life he had prayed for the opportunity to sanctify God's name in public by dying with the last breath of his life proclaiming the unity of God. How could he not do so now that he was granted his wish? Similarly, the young soldiers of the Jewish liberation army of the forties, asked how they could not die now for the liberty of their people and their land, after struggling all their lives for the moment when they could do so. Avshalom Chaviv, Yaakov Weiss and Meir Nekker looked upon their impending execution not as a tragedy, but as a fulfillment of their dream to serve and demonstrate their loyalty to God, the Jewish people and the Jewish land. To them their death was a vindication of their faith and the ultimate proof of their fidelity to their cause. It was not a sacrifice. It was a privilege.

The episode from the period of the Spanish Expulsion is this. There was a Jewish mother who had two sons who were killed. After their death she offered a prayer in which she said, "Master of the universe, until now I loved you, but not completely because I also had two children to love and shared my love for You with my love for them. Now, however, my heart is entirely freed, emptied of any other love, to be a vessel solely for love for You." After concluding the tale of this great heroine of Jewish Motherhood, the three modern prisoners of Zion, Avshalom Chaviv, Yaakov Weiss and Meir Nekker, said, "We are ready to leave room in our parents' hearts to love the land and the people of our God in our place"! One of their visitors concludes his report of this profoundly moving exchange saying, "I looked at them in silence. What was I to say to them? 'My sons,' I said at last, 'go to your father Abraham.' "

Indeed what can we add to this story of Jewish commitment to and sacrifice for God, people and country.

They accepted death as the ultimate virtue of life and opportunity to serve God. But this nobility of soul and spirit did not come to them from a vacuum. It emanated from their bottomless faith in their cause and in God. In the face of this tremendous faith death was no threat. It was only a challenge that they gladly met head on. God was not a silent bystander. He was a witness to their courage, faith and purity of purpose and innocence of motive. To them the statement from *Shabbath* 88b applies; the rabbis taught, those [people] who are disgraced but do not disgrace other [people], listen to how they are being dishonored and do not respond, and they who fulfill [God's commandments] out of love and rejoice in their own suffering, of them it is written, "Those who love Him are like the sun at its height" (Judges 5).

The lives of martyrs of our time, like the martyrs in the days of the Expulsion from Spain and the days of Rabbi Akiva, were like the sun at its highest. They did what they had to do with faith in their souls, love in their hearts, steadfast commitments in their minds to the noble ideals of God, Torah and the Jewish people. To this, God Himself bears testimony. *Chagigah* 13b states, "Rabbi Yehudah said in the name of Rav, Why did God allow the evil Nebuchadnezar to conquer the entire world? He did so in order that the nations of the world should not say that God handed over His children into the hands of a lowly people." The very power and might that the British, the Germans, the Romans and the ancient Greeks represented was in and of itself a testament to the nobility and greatness of the Jewish people. It elevated the martyrdom of the Jews then and now to a level of religious righteousness, moral rectitude and spiritual splendor.

That is not to minimize the tragedy of their suffering and death. On the contrary, it is to heighten it. Indeed, as it was said, "Only through a sense of tragedy is it possible to be instructed by the past."

—CR

23

A Ray of Light
from the Past upon the Present

In an age when it is popular to question the ways of God, particularly when it comes to the terrible events of the *Shoah*, it may be enlightening and helpful to learn how our mothers and fathers of a bygone age have faced adversity and horrendous torture and pain both personally and in the face of their dear ones.

The Talmud, tractate *Avoda Zara* 19a, relates how the biblical verse, "The Rock, His work is perfect; For all His ways are justice; A God of faithfulness and without iniquity. Just and right is He" (Deuteronomy 32:34), is interpreted in the time of the tragic murder of the family of Rabbi Chanina ben Tradyon, who was one of the Ten Martyrs of the Faith during the Hadrianic persecution of the Jews in the first half of the second century of the common era.

This is the context in which the passage was interpreted: "When Rabbi Chanina ben Tradyon, his wife and daughter were taken to be burned at the stake," the Talmud tells us, "they justified God's decree that was to befall them." Rabbi Chanina said: "The Rock His work is perfect; For all His ways are justice." His wife said: "A God of faithfulness and without iniquity; Just and right is He." His daughter said: "Great in council and mighty in work; Whose eyes are open upon all the ways of the sons of men, to give every one according to his ways, and according to the fruit of his doing" (Jeremiah 32:19).

What a powerful message Rabbi Chanina, his wife and daughter send us via the pages of the Talmud. They do not tell us how horrible their pain and torture was. Instead they tell us how God is not to blame for their suffering. What a courageous way of assuming oneself the responsibility for what happens to one and not putting the blame on someone else, namely God. How unlike our own age when everything that befalls one, banal or brutal in nature, is always blamed on God or society. Instead they hasten to vindicate God and His ways lest anyone rise to blame Him for their suffering. In the eyes of Rabbi Chanina and his family God, is always just. If we encounter problems of any magnitude, even though they take our life, we should not complain. Like Rabbi Chanina, his wife and daughter, we should accept with love whatever God brings our way. No one can question the extent of their suffering! They paid the ultmate price! They earned the right to have an opinion and to be heard when they express that opinion on what it means to suffer. Suffering is brought upon us by ourselves. It is not God's fault but ours. We should examine our ways and not blame God.

How different is their view from that of Emerson, one of the shapers of American thinking, who said,

> The ways of Providence are inscrutable
> It is often wild and rough
> And it is of no use to try to whitewash its huge,
> mixed instrumentalities.

It is not a question of whitewashing God's intrumentalities or a matter of accusing God of using wild and rough ways in dealing with mankind. It is rather a matter of assuming the responsibility for the events that mold the destiny of humankind, and looking within ourselves for the troubles that befall humanity. The same applies to the lot of the Jewish people and its perception of the unfathomable tragedy in the annals of recorded history that we call the *Shoah*.

The Talmud, tractate *Brachot*, states that "One should bless the name of God for the bad just as well as for the good things that happen to us." Rabbi Chanina and his family did just that. It may not be too late to start talking and thinking about the *Shoah* in the same spirit.

—*CR*

24

The Number of Jewish Children

Full statistics of the number of children who died during the Holocaust will never be known. Some estimates range as high as one and a half million murdered children. This figure includes more than one million two-hundred thousand Jewish children, tens of thousands of Gypsy children, and thousands of institutionalized handicapped children who were murdered under Nazi rule in Germany and occupied Europe. Although children were seldom the targets of Nazi violence because they were children, they were persecuted along with their families for racial, religious or political reasons. Chances of survival were somewhat higher for older children, since they could potentially be assigned to forced labor in concentration camps and ghettos.

The Jews were a special target of the Nazi ideology that ultimately resulted in the Holocaust and the systematic state-sponsored murder of six million European Jews. From the very first, Jews and their children suffered at the hands of the Nazis and thus the world of Jewish children was rapidly restricted as soon as the Nazis came to power in Germany in January 1933. Even before 1939, when World War Two started, many German Jewish children had no chance of emigrating even as German society grew increasingly hostile. After 1935, as Nazi propaganda increasingly vilified Jews in movies, books and newspapers, close friends suddenly avoided the company of their Jewish classmates, sometimes becoming openly hostile. In addition, there was humiliation that confronted Jewish and Gypsy children in German classrooms, as teachers instructed their students in Nazi beliefs that Jews and Gypsies were inferior races.

Laws were passed that restricted Jews from attending educational institutions. For example, there was a law that stated that the Jewish population could not exceed 1.5 percent of the total number of students. Jewish children of war veterans and those with a non-Jewish parent were initially exempted. Later decrees escalated in intensity and shortly after the November 1938 pogrom also known as *Kristalnacht*—The Night of the Broken Glass. German Jewish children were prohibited from attending German schools. This same measure also excluded Gypsy children from German schools. Conditions steadily deteriorated as Nazi pressure increased, and on July 7, 1942, Jewish schools were finally closed after the first wave of deportations of German Jews to the East had been completed. After 1938, schooling of Gypsy children was not of serious concern to Nazi authorities. First in Germany and later in occupied Europe, the Jewish experiences of persecution affected children. The world of childhood and adolescence, usually a time of testing and experimentation, became instead a world of shrinking horizons after 1933. For example, German Jewish children were systematically driven from the wider German society, creating a community in which Jews were isolated. Jews could no longer belong to the same clubs and social organizations as Aryan children; they were banned from using public recreational facilities and playgrounds and were also vulnerable to the traumas of loss and separation from their homes and familiar surroundings. However, a few thousand German and Austrian Jewish children were able to escape the Nazi net, since they were sent abroad in "Kindertransports" to the Netherlands, Great Britain, Palestine, and the United States before 1939. With the onset of war, Jewish children in occupied Poland and later throughout Europe were confined with their families in overcrowded ghettos and transit camps, exposed to malnutrition, disease, exposure, and early death. Gypsy and handicapped children were similarly categorized in Nazi Germany and occupied Europe by race and biology. By July 1933 the Nazi quest for a biologically pure society included the Law to Prevent Offspring with Hereditary Defects. In ever escalating legislation, mentally and physically handicapped children were vulnerable to sterilization prior to 1939, and to murder in the so-called euthanasia program after 1939. Eugenic and racial measures also extended to six hundred German mulatto children (the offspring of German women and African French colonial troops occupying the Rhineland in the 1920s). These Afro-German children were registered by the Gestapo and Interior Ministry in 1937 and they were all brutally sterilized in German university hospitals that same year. The methods of children's euthanasia were developed between February and May 1939. First, the physicians and Nazi officials registered their potential victims. These registration forms, called Meldebogen, collected data from midwives and physicians, who reported all infants born with specific medical conditions. The first killings of children in special wards by overdoses of poison occurred in October 1939. Parents who attempted to remove their children from the killing wards were rarely able to succeed. With fathers already absent as soldiers, mothers who disagreed were often assigned to contractual labor, thereby necessitating the commitment of handicapped children in state institutions. The killing of disabled children marked the beginning of the euthanasia program and continued throughout the war. Children's euthanasia was central to the program, because children represented the future, and the Nazi physicians considered the elimination of those they considered diseased and deformed as essential to their aim of racial purification. Although it is impossible to calculate with certainty the number of children killed in these special children's wards during World War II, the best estimate is that at least five thousand German and Austrian children were killed in these programs. Nazi persecution, arrests and deportations were directed against all members of Jewish families, as well as many Gypsy families, without concern for age. Inevitably the children were among the prisoners at highest risk. Homeless, often orphaned, they had frequently witnessed the murder of parents, siblings and relatives. They faced starvation, illness, brutal labor and other indignities until they were consigned to the gas chambers. In comparison to adult prisoners, their chances for survival were usually smaller although their adaptability to radically changed circumstances could sometimes increase the odds in their favor. That these Jewish children survived at all and also created diaries, poems, and drawings in virtually all ghettos and concentration camps is truly remarkable. After 1939, there are four basic patterns that can describe the fate of both Jewish and non-Jewish children in occupied Europe: (1) Those killed immediately on arrival in concentration camps and killing centers; (2) those killed shortly after birth (for example, the 870 infants born in the Ravensbruck concentration camp, largely to Jewish and Gypsy women, between 1943 and 1945); (3) those born in ghettos and camps and surviving; (4) and those children, usually above the age of ten, utilized as prisoners, laborers, and subjects for horrible Nazi medical experiments. Thus, of the fifteen thousand children imprisoned in the Theresiensdadt Ghetto, only about one thousand one hundred survived. Children sometimes also survived in hiding and also participated in the resistance, as runners, messengers and smugglers. In retrospect, Hitler's intention to exterminate the Jewish nation was preceded by many programs involving the most vulnerable population of German society, such as the mentally retarded and the children of mixed racial backgrounds. If Germans of good conscience had fought to stop these programs from being implemented, perhaps the terrible fate that awaited six million Jews could have been averted.

—BR

25

Where Was America?

Imagine for a moment that you are a Jew living in Germany in 1939. The outward displays of anti-semitism have made life extraordinarily uncomfortable, and since Hitler has already offered Jews the chance to vacate the country, you and your family are seriously thinking of leaving. To your delight, your parents announce that they will be relocating the family to the "great land of opportunity"—America—where the streets are paved with gold and everyone is welcome. You and your family sell all of your possessions, and purchase tickets for the long journey across the Atlantic to the "land of liberty, justice, and equality for all."

But what happens? After the long, arduous voyage, the boat is turned away. The American immigration officers report that the quotas have been filled. "What quotas?" you think. Surely America would not turn away the tired, hungry, and persecuted Jews who are knocking at its door! The United States Coast Guard boats prevent your ship from reaching the mainland, and the miserable would-be immigrants are rejected without even a glimpse at the wonderful land of America, but not without a glance at potential freedom. But the worst has not happened . . . it is yet to come. Your ship is forced to wander, looking for other ports . . . it may be destroyed en route by a wandering German U-boat, or forced make the hazardous journey back across the ocean to ports in Europe. . . . you would be free for the moment, only to be caught later by the Nazis and killed, or worse, to be put in a concentration camp.

Such is the story of countless Jews, all of whom flocked to ships that would ferry them across the great ocean to the Land of Endless Wealth, only to be turned away, to other oversea ports, or sent back to Germany or German-occupied countries, where they would be eventually captured. Germany allowed Jews to leave until 1941, and until then, some European countries accepted Jews, and hid them: Poland, France, Belgium, the Netherlands, and Denmark all served as hiding places, and some served as havens for refugee Jews during the Holocaust. Some Jews hid until the war's end, but many, many more were rooted out and killed by the Nazis. The few places that they would have been safe were overseas, especially the United States of America, which alone could have saved more than half of those six million souls that perished by the black hand of the Nazis. Although the United States could have saved numerous lives, they did not. Unfortunately, this was because the nation was fiercely anti-Semitic, and forced their sentiments into national politics and foreign policy. America did not like foreigners, and especially did not like Jewish foreigners. The effects of this racism were not visible to Americans until long after the war's end. From 1933 to 1941, opponents of refugee immigration had built their case around the high unemployment of the Great Depression. Restrictionists stubbornly asserted that refugees that came to the United States usurped jobs that rightfully belonged to unemployed American workers. Their viewpoint was widely accepted, and the counter argument, that refugees were consumers as well as the workers, and thus provided as many jobs as they took, had little success. Economic pressure against immigration had been reinforced by strong feelings of nativism, or "one-hundred percent Americanism." This intolerance, which had run very high in the aftermath of World War I, had combined with economic forces during the 1920's to install the quota system, the nation's first wide restriction of immigration. The quotas set specific limits on the number of people who could immigrate to the United States in any given year from any given foreign country. The annual total of all quotas was 154,000 persons, more than half of which was allocated to countries that had no need to send refugees. In the 1930's, anti-alien attitudes had played a major part in keeping refugee immigration to low levels. The United States lowered its quota barriers in 1938, but began raising them again in autumn of 1939. Two years later, immigration was even more tightly restricted than before in 1938. In fact, starting in July 1941, America's gates were nearly shut. The best chance to save the European Jews had passed. In 1941, with the Holocaust well underway, the need for help became acute. By then, though, saving Jews was much more difficult. Determined rescue efforts would be needed to salvage even a segment of European Jewry, and the United States took no interest in rescue efforts until 1944, and even then the attempt was limited. America still refused to open its gates, and immigration was held to about ten percent of its already small quota limits. The last chance to help

European Jews had come and gone. In the years before Pearl Harbor, the United States had reacted to the European Jewish crisis with some concern, but had refused to permit any sizable immigration of refugees. This policy grew out of three aspects of American society in the 1930's: unemployment, nativistic restrictionism, and anti-semitism, and was shaped by Congress and the Roosevelt Administration. Even after Pearl Harbor, the war itself narrowed the possibilities for saving Jews, for America was more interested in winning the war than it was in saving the war's victims. In addition, the mass media's reluctance to draw attention to Holocaust developments undermined efforts to create significant public pressure for government rescue action. But the deeper causes for the lateness and weakness of America's attempts at rescue, and for its unwillingness to take in more than a tiny trickle of fleeing Jews, were essentially the same ones that had determined the nation's reaction to the refugee crisis before Pearl Harbor, that is, a strong sense of American nativism, and an even stronger sense of anti-semitism. Wartime prosperity in America did not dissolve the economic argument against immigration, as one would expect. Fear was widespread that the Depression would return at the war's end. Millions believed that the demobilization of the armed forces and return to a peacetime economy would cause an extended period of large-scale unemployment. Veterans' organizations were especially forceful in insisting on the protection of employment rights for returning soldiers. In their view, every foreigner allowed into the country meant job competition for the American citizenry. Throughout the war, the American Legion and the Veterans of Foreign Wars demanded a virtual ban on immigration. Siding with these groups were the Daughters of the American Revolution and the American Coalition of Patriotic Societies. The anti-immigration forces wielded significant political power, and made it very difficult for American Jews to rouse any public compassion for their European brethren. Moreover, a number of congressmen were resolutely restrictionist, a reflection of their own views as well as of the attitudes that pervaded their home districts. Most of them were anti-alien with a passion that drifted into anti-Semitism. It was not only the politicians who were anti-alien, but the citizenry as well. America's limited willingness to share the refugee burden showed clearly in national opinion polls. In 1938, while the Nazis were intensifying Jewish persecution, four separate polls indicated that seventy-one percent to eighty-five percent of the American public was against an increase of quotas to help refugees, and sixty-seven percent wanted refugees out altogether. In a survey taken in 1939, sixty-six percent objected to a one-time exception to allow ten thousand refugee children to enter outside quota limits. Even in 1944, in the midst of the war, seventy-eight percent said that it would be a bad idea to let immigrants into the country after the war, and in 1945, after the war, when all of the horrors of the Holocaust were widely known, only five percent said that the United States should let in more immigrants than they did before the war, and a shocking fourteen percent said that they should send all the refugees back to where they came from! While it is obvious that many who opposed refugee immigration felt no love for Jews, much restrictionist and anti-refugee sentiment was closely linked to real anti-semitism. The plain truth is that many Americans were prejudiced against Jews and were unlikely to support measures to help them. Before Pearl Harbor, anti-semitism had shaped American policy, and afterwards, it hardened Americans toward the victims of the Holocaust. American anti-semitism, which had climbed to very high levels in the late 1930's, continued to rise in the first part of the 1940's. It reached its historic peak in 1944. By spring 1942, sociologist David Reisman was describing it as "slightly below boiling point," and three years later, public opinion expert Elmo Roper warned that "anti-semitism has spread all over the nation and is particularly virulent in urban centers."

For every Jew America didn't allow into the country, another human being was killed. If there was less hate and fear in America, perhaps millions of Jews could have been saved.

—BR

26

Righteous Gentiles
during the Holocaust

The Holocaust is one of the darkest periods in the history of the Jewish people. We hear about the gas chambers, the forced labor, the starvation, and the indescribable horror of all that occurred. How could people have stooped to such a low level of humanity as to actually have committed such terrible atrocities, we ask ourselves, especially during the twentieth century—an era of supposed tolerance and enlightenment. Where was the world when six million Jews, including one and a half million children, perished at the hands of the Nazis? We ask ourselves these questions and unfortunately, we have no ready answers.

Where was the world and why did so few people attempt to assist the Jews in their time of need? However, not all non-Jews living at the time took part in the hatred against and the killing of the Jews. We should not undermine the importance of the actions of those righteous Gentiles who actually did risk and even sacrifice their own lives in order to save Jewish lives. We should keep in mind what courage these individuals displayed, especially considering the hostility of their surroundings at that time.

The early 1930s ushered in a period of tremendous crusades against the Jews, when propaganda promoted prejudice and hate as acceptable or even praiseworthy, and when the government itself began to maintain a policy of rampant discrimination against Jews and other non-Aryans. In spite of all this, however, there were those individuals who still maintained a sense of virtue. During a time when almost everyone around them was on an all-out campaign against the Jews, many righteous Gentiles refused to take part in the hatred and anti-semitism. To the contrary, these individuals gathered their courage and took action to help save Jewish lives. Even though many did remain silent about what was happening, there were those who did not allow themselves to disregard the plight of the Jews.

The road leading up to Yad Va Shem, the Holocaust Memorial in Israel, is called the "Avenue of the Righteous," and is lined with trees planted to acknowledge and commemorate the heroic acts of these individuals, who have come to be known as the *Chasidei Umot Haolam*—the righteous Gentiles. Who knows, were it not for these good people, if all the Jews would not have been murdered? Who can tell, maybe these good people were really God's messengers to save the remnant of His people? Many of these people are well-known names and have had movies made or books written about their stories; others are not so well-known. But it is extremely important for us to give recognition to those who deserve it and to discuss the efforts of the righteous Gentiles, who helped save thousands of Jewish lives.

Most of the time, the non-Jews who helped save Jews did so either by bringing them into hiding or by helping them escape to a neutral country. Many also hid the Jews in their own homes during the entire war. The most famous story about those who went into hiding is that of Anne Frank and her family. In 1941, when Otto Frank saw Jews being rounded up and he began to realize what was taking place, he made plans to bring his family into hiding. "He had been forced to leave his business, but his Dutch associates and employees remained loyal friends." Otto Frank decided to bring his family to the secret annex, a group of rooms located at the top and back of one of his office buildings.

Without the help of four friends of the family who worked downstairs, Mr. Koophuis, Mr. Kraler, Elli Vossen, and Miep Van Santen, the Frank family never could have remained hidden for as long as they did, avoiding detection for three years. These four people kept the family's whereabouts a secret, brought them food and other items, and relayed to them reports of the events taking place in the city. By doing this, they placed themselves in grave danger, as they were going against strict Nazi orders, which forbade anyone to have contact with a Jewish person. Ultimately, when the Frank family was reported to the Gestapo by a Dutch informer and sent to a concentration camp, Mr. Koophuis and Mr. Kraler were taken as prisoners as well. Mr. Koophuis was released for medical treatment, but Mr. Kraler was forced to spend eight months in a labor camp, under strenuous conditions.

Another Dutch citizen responsible for saving Jewish lives was Joop Westerwill, a courageous and noble man who helped hundreds of Jewish children and teenagers escape the Nazis. Mr. Westerwill was the principal of a school in Rotterdam when Germany invaded the Netherlands. He began to rent apartments in his own name in order to provide Jewish families with places to stay. He would also help smuggle Jews out of the country. For twenty months Joop did his lifesaving work, sometimes sleeping only two hours a night, because by day he continued to work as principal of the school.

On March 11, 1944, Mr. Westerwill was captured by the Nazis and brought to jail, where he was constantly beaten and tortured. In August 1944, he was shot by the Nazis.

The people of Le Chambon, a small village in the mountains of southern France, were able to band together and save almost 5,000 Jews. "The pastor's house was a stopping off point for refugees who passed through the town. Then a team of men took them across the mountains to Switzerland." Similarly, the whole country of Denmark refused to take part in the collaboration against the Jews. Instead, they banded together in an effort to transport almost the entire Jewish population across the border to Sweden. All in all, the Danish citizens managed to heroically save the lives of over eight thousand Jews.

Another possible way to prevent Jews from being sent to the death camps was to take them in as workers. The movie *Schindler's List* portrays the courageous actions of factory owner, Oskar Schindler, who began to employ Jews to work in his enamelware factory. He was constantly bribing German officials in order to keep these Jews in his factory. Although food was scarce, he did everything possible to feed "his Jews" and provide them with a safe place to live. When Schindler learned that he would have to give up his Jewish workers for relocation, meaning extermination, he used his influence to transfer his entire factory to Czechoslovakia, at great personal risk. Today, thousands of Jews owe their lives to the bravery of Oskar Schindler. Another individual who saved hundreds of Jews by giving them employment was a German engineer by the name of Hans Fritz Graebe. At times, he would see killing units gathering up Jews to be shot and this impelled him to try to do even more to save Jews from this plight.

Another righteous Gentile, Raoul Wallenberg, a Swedish

diplomat, issued Swedish passports to twenty thousand Jews and created shelters for eight thousand children. In addition, when he heard that a Jewish ghetto populated by seventy thousand Jews was to be destroyed, he risked his life by threatening the Nazi commander in charge of these plans. Since it was near the end of the war, the German retreated. In this manner, Raoul Wallenberg managed to save almost one hundred thousand Jewish lives. Amidst all of the horror stories and accounts of the atrocities that occurred during the Holocaust, we find many inspiring accounts of courage and resistance.

I, Chaim Rozwaski, bear personal witness to the fact that some Gentiles risked their and their families' lives to hide Jews and help them survive the war. I and my aunt, my father's, of blessed memory, sister-in-law, and her two daughters, my cousins, lived with a farmer in order to hide from the Germans and their cohorts. I stayed on the farm for about three to four months. They stayed for about two years until it became impossible to remain there any longer because the neighboring farmers were beginning to talk about the farmer having Jews on his farm. At that point my aunt and her daughters joined us in the partisans. Shortly thereafter, the farmer and his son, Andrey, (I remember him well, he was particularly nice to me), were shot and killed by the Germans. They were the victims of their own neighbors who informed on them.

I also remember other farmers who gave us food and even some clothing to wear. I remember a particularly tall lady farmer who brought us food, mainly potatoes, while we were hiding in a small grove near her house. We came to that place the day after we escaped by the grace of God from our town when all the Jews were slaughtered. We stayed in that grove for twenty-one days. (For some reason I remember that number clearly.) My uncle, Shlomo, would go to her house at night pretending that we were far away and that he walked half the night to get to her house for the food, because we were afraid that she might inform on us. All the time she acted as though she accepted what he said at face value. We were both shocked and surprised when on the day before we left that little grove we called a forest, in order to go to the really big forest known as Lipitchanskaya Push'tcha, she showed up at our encampment to say good-bye to us and wish us well. We were shocked because we realized how exposed and vulnerable we were, while all the time she, and therefore maybe other farmers, also knew where we were hiding. We were surprised and happy because we realized that we really had a good friend in her. What's more, she refused to take any money from us for the food she gave us. And yet, we were suspicious and apprehensive, not being sure of her real motives and thinking. We kept on the lookout the moment she left us, because we were afraid she might inform on us. So great was our fear and so all-encompassing and deep was the threat to our lives from every person around us, that we could not even enjoy the simple pleasure of a woman who meant us no harm and only came to help us! We remained in a state of apprehension and fear during the long and hot summer day that seemed endless until well into the night when it was dark, and we could set out on the road to the faraway forest and the unknown that lay ahead in store for us.

There were many more people who helped. Alas, there were too few of them. But those who did will receive their just reward in Heaven.

It is extremely important for us to recognize and to pay tribute to the Gentiles who, during the Holocaust, did not just turn their backs to what was happening but, at the risk of death, helped save Jewish people. We now tend to believe that too few individuals tried to help and that more could have been done to save the Jews. However, we should keep in mind the fact that, by becoming involved with assisting Jews, a non-Jew living under the Nazi government stood to be sentenced to death or to a concentration camp, sometimes considered a fate worse than death. In a time when so many around them were engaged in anti-semitism and ruthless murder, these righteous Gentiles clung to their morals and fought courageously to help the Jews. A quote from the Gemarah so accurately sums up the extent of the heroism of these individuals: "He who saves a single life, it is as though he has saved the world entire."[1]

—BR, CR

---

[1] *Sanhedrin* 37a.

About the Authors

Rabbi Bernhard H. Rosenberg, the only child of Holocaust survivors Jacob and Rachel, of blessed memory, is the rabbi of Congregation Beth El in Edison, NJ. Rabbi Rosenberg serves as the interfaith chairman of the New Jersey State Holocaust Commission and is the associate editor of the Holocaust curriculum for the State of New Jersey. He is the founder of the State of New Jersey Children of the Holocaust Organization. His other books include *Theological and Halachic Reflections of the Holocaust* and a *Guide for the Jewish Mourner*. He received his ordination and doctoral degree from Yeshiva University. Rabbi Rosenberg has taught at Yeshiva University and Rutgers University, and currently teaches Holocaust studies at the Moshe Aaron Yeshiva of Central New Jersey. He regularly appears on radio and television, and his articles appear in numerous magazines and newspapers throughout the country. Rabbi Rosenberg resides in Edison, NJ, with his wife Charlene and their four children, Ilana, Ayelet, Yaakov, and Ari.

Chaim Z. Rozwaski is the founding dean of the Lauder Jüdisches Lehrhaus in Berlin. He is also the rabbi of the Ryke Strasse Synagogue in Berlin. Rabbi Rozwaski previously served as rabbi of the Suburban Park Jewish Center, Congregation Lev Torah in East Meadow, NY. He received ordination from the Hebrew Theological College in 1962 and has served as the spiritual leader of congregations in the United States and England. Born in Poland, Rabbi Rozwaski survived the Holocaust with his aunt and uncle by hiding with partisans in the forest. He has been very active in Jewish organizations, particularly in the areas of the Holocaust, the United Jewish Appeal, and Israel Bonds. His work has garnered him such recognition as being invited to the White House by President Jimmy Carter for the signing of the Camp David peace accord, and the establishment of the Holocaust Memorial Center. Twice he delivered the opening prayer at the United States House of Representatives. The recipient of a doctorate in Talmudic Law from the Ner Israel Rabbinical College in Baltimore, MD, he also holds a master's degree in philosophy and education from Purdue University in Indiana. Rabbi Rozwaski has published articles in many magazines, including *Judaism*, *The Jewish Spectator*, and *Midstream*. He resides with his wife, Roberta, in Berlin.